WAR AND FLAMES
1939 – 1946

by Pat Moseley

Printed by
Clarke Printing, Monmouth

Published by Pat Jones-Jenkins

Copyright © Pat Moseley

ISBN 978-0-9561464-0-3

WAR AND FLAMES
1939 – 1946

Compiled by Pat Moseley and members of Rudry Local History Group from conversations with 'Ruperra' soldiers in many parts of the British Isles, with local people and their friends and relatives in the 1980s and 90s and from photos and documents donated by them

Printed by Clarke Printing, Monmouth

DEDICATIONS AND CREDITS

This book was compiled in 2001 to commemorate the sixtieth anniversary of the burning down of Ruperra Castle on December 6th 1941. It is dedicated to all those who knew Ruperra in the dark days of World War Two, most of whom are no longer with us, and to those of us who remember them and who deeply desire to keep their memory alive and with it the sacrifices they made for us.

Acknowledgements

The Mobile Field Bakery plates are made available by John Rogers of the 37th Mobile Bakery and are acknowledged as follows:
"© Crown Copyright 1942/MOD. Reproduced with the permission of Her Majesty's Stationery Office."

The RAF aerial photograph "© Crown Copyright 1954 Reproduced with the permission of Her Majesty's Stationery Office
The other aerial photographs are by courtesy of Terence Soames Photography.

The newspaper article is reproduced by courtesy of the South Wales Argus.

All the remaining photographs used in the book are donated either by the people whose accounts appear in this book or by their relatives or friends.

The cover design is by Chris Jones-Jenkins.

Other books about Ruperra include:
 'Lord Tredegar's Ruperra Castle'
        by Tony Friend (1985) A short history with many pictures.
 'Memories of Coed Craig Ruperra'
        compiled by Pat Moseley from audio tape recordings (1999)
 'Serving under Ruperra'
        compiled by Pat Moseley from recordings of people who worked on the Ruperra Estate in the first half of the 20th century.

How this book came about.

In 1985 members of the newly formed Rudry Local History Group, fascinated by the ruined Ruperra Castle and its beautiful estate, started to make audio tape recordings of local people with Ruperra connections. They were eventually directed to Mrs May Pembridge, who had returned to live in her home town of Llandyssyl on the death of her husband. Once a servant at the Castle herself, and with some interesting recollections, she had among her papers a list that her husband Tom had made, recording the army units stationed and trained at the Castle during the Second World War. Tom had been right hand man to many at the Castle and had been caretaker while the soldiers were there and afterwards.

As the years went by, the task of capturing the soldiers' reminiscences became more urgent. Local soldiers were fairly easy to locate and record, and people came forward with information and with their own reminiscences at each Ruperra Conservation Trust exhibition held around the area. After being kindly allowed to have a stall at one of the 'Machen Remembered' exhibitions, I was inundated with responses.

A letter to Tony Friend, whose book, published in 1985, had greatly encouraged interest in the Castle, solved once and for all the question of which unit was stationed in the Castle when it burnt down on the night of December 6th, 1941. It sent me off to Tyneside on the first of several journeys around the country to meet and record the memories of the 'Ruperra soldiers'. Having advertised in 'Legion', the Royal British Legion Magazine, the responses took me to meet soldiers in Cheshire, Southampton, Deal, Gillingham, Penzance, Edmonton, Edgware and Buntingsford, not to mention those living nearer at hand.

The quest for the firemen who attended the fire at the Castle was not so successful. Generally older than the soldiers, which was why they were not away fighting, they are no longer with us. Only Henry Whitnell from Caerphilly, who had been a seventeen year old fire station messenger boy that night, was still alive. Sadly, he too has now passed away.

Published sixty years on, this book was a means of thanking all the Ruperra soldiers for the sacrifices that they made in World War Two. I remember, as a little girl, the feel of the rough, hard and unyielding texture of my father's RAF uniform. It was symbolic of an alien force over which families had no control. When you hugged the wearer of the uniform to say 'goodbye', you knew that he had to go. You just hoped he would come back. All the Ruperra soldiers I spoke to were home loving kindly men sent out on an undesired mission to kill others.

I would like to thank all who have contributed their recollections and those who found old photographs and documents and willingly passed them on to me. There are too many to name individually but their generosity reflects their belief that the events of those momentous years should not be forgotten.

I also want to take this opportunity to mention the success of the Coed Craig Ruperra Woodland project. Congratulations and thanks must be extended to the members of Ruperra Conservation Trust and the 'Friends of Ruperra', to all those members of the public who donated money and all the public charitable bodies who made funds and support available, including Caerphilly County Borough Council. Their faith has made our woodland project at Ruperra a reality. Coed Craig Ruperra, the 'hill of pears' will now be safeguarded as a green island of unspoilt countryside, commanding the same view of the sea and far off hills as our ancestors once saw. It will be a fitting memorial for the soldiers at the Castle.

Pat Moseley, October 2001

Websites:
> Main trust: www.ruperra.org.uk
> Castle campaign: www.ruperracastle.blogspot.com

Some of the local Ruperra soldiers are pictured here at a reunion at Machen United Services Club. The kindness of Mr Reg Leewarden, Mrs Phyllis Jones and Mrs Janet Sargeant of the British Legion Club, helped to make an enjoyable occasion. From the right anti clockwise, Roy Reeves Gordon Crooke, Andy Newton, Stan Lavery Frank Baumer and South Wales Echo reporter, Wendy Horton.

CONTENTS

Tom Pembridge's Records

1939 24th November Signals came to Ruperra   38th Div
Left 23rd/24th June 1940

1940 24th June Bakers came to Ruperra   3rd and 4th Field Bakery
Left 7th July 1940

1940 7th July 2nd Field Bakery came to Ruperra
Left 18th August 1940

1940 29th August Dutch soldiers came to Ruperra
Left 10th October 1940

1940 10th October RAMC Advance Party   199 Field Ambulance
18th RAMC and RASC
Left 15th February 1941

1941 15th February 152 Field Ambulance

1941 3rd May Indians attached to F.A.
A Coy. and 15 HG and B. Left August 8th, C Coy Left September 1st

1941 November 16th Fatigue Party came.
Left November 21st

1941 November 21st Advance Party Searchlights
23rd November 307th Searchlights
Left December 15th on a Saturday 5.45

1941 December 6th Castle burnt down

1942 March 20th March 20th Bakery came to Ruperra 37th MFB
August 18th Americans attached to 37th MFB

[There is a gap here in Tom Pembridge's records. We know that in 1944 there were bakery training units at Ruperra]

1946 July 9th   Bakery and Germans left Ruperra.

Overleaf : Aerial views of Ruperra in 2002 and 2007

1

2

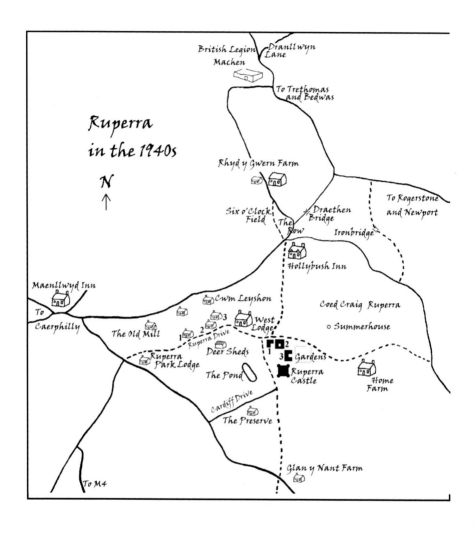

Ruperra
in the 1940s
N
↑

British Legion
Machen

Dranllwyn
Lane

To Trethomas
and Bedwas

Rhyd y Gwern Farm

To Rogerstone
and Newport

Six o'Clock
Field

Draethen
Bridge

The
Row

Ironbridge

Hollybush Inn

Maenllwyd Inn

To
Caerphilly

Cwm Leyshon

Coed Craig Ruperra

o Summerhouse

West
Lodge

The Old Mill

1   2   3

Ruperra Drive

Deer Sheds

2
1
3   Garden3

Ruperra
Park Lodge

The Pond

Ruperra
Castle

Home
Farm

Cardiff Drive

The Preserve

To M4

Glan y Nant Farm

INTRODUCTION

The Ruperra Estate, part of the huge Tredegar Estates, which once covered 53,000 acres in South East Wales, is situated in beautiful open rolling countryside between Cardiff, Caerphilly and Newport. The Morgan family who lived at Tredegar House in Newport, used the Castle, built by their ancestor Thomas Morgan in 1626, only as a country residence in later years, although their children and the heirs to the Tredegar Estates had been brought up there. By the 1920s however the fortunes of the family were declining, and in 1933 the Ruperra Estate was put up for sale. No Morgan had been in residence since the death in 1913 of Godfrey, Lord Tredegar, of 'Charge of the Light Brigade' fame. His nephew Courtenay, who had lived partly at Ruperra since the death of his father Colonel Freddie in 1909, moved to Tredegar House as the new Lord Tredegar. A skeleton staff kept the estate and the beautiful gardens in good order and provided for the needs of family weekend shooting and hunting parties.

Ruperra Castle view from the east in the 1930s.

Courtney loved Ruperra Castle, however, having lived there as a boy, and spent a great deal of money on improvements to the buildings and gardens to entice his son Evan to live at the castle when he married.

But Evan didn't enjoy hunting and shooting. He liked painting and poetry and preferred to live in Paris and London. After his father died in 1934 the Ruperra Estate was put up for sale. The Morgan family had suffered three deaths in a short space of time, with the attendant death duties. Also they had not found a way to modernise their farming methods so as to withstand the effects of the economic depression of the 20s and 30s. The Tredegar Estate managers were optimistic that Ruperra would prove attractive to buyers eager to make the estate into a going concern once again. But there were no offers.

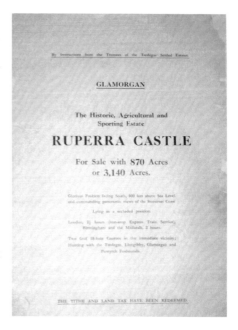

The Cover of the Sale Brochure of 1934

In the following November 1935 the contents of the Castle were sold. What was left was taken to Tredegar House for safekeeping. An even more depleted skeleton staff was retained to look after the Castle, the outbuildings and parkland. Gamekeepers Mr. Rae and Albert Blackburn were two of them and another was Tom Pembridge. He lived on the estate, tending the generators and acting as caretaker until the estate was finally sold in 1955.

The sale of the contents of the castle would have seemed like the end of the world for the old Head Gardener, Angus McKinnon but he had died in May 1935, a year after his wife, Agnes. His gravestone in Lower Machen Churchyard says simply, 'Angus McKinnon of Ruperra Castle Gardens'.

This little book describes the effects of the Second World War on the fortunes and future of Ruperra and on the lives of the people who had once been intimately bound up with it. It also describes the impression that Ruperra made on some of the soldiers who were billeted at the Castle, the changes that the war made to the lives of the village people around, and significantly, the tragic burning down of the Castle on the night of December 6 1941.

The reactions of the soldiers who came to live in this large stately home were very varied. Those soldiers who came forward with their memories enjoyed telling them, and their recollection of details after so many years was truly remarkable. For me, the various eyewitness accounts and theories about responsibility for the fire have added to the fascination of this journey of discovery.

One soldier spent just one night at Ruperra Castle a few weeks after it burnt down. Having never heard anything more about it, he had always wondered what happened. When a neighbour told him about an advert I had put in the British Legion magazine to find more Ruperra soldiers, he took the opportunity to find out. He was amazed to learn that the Castle was still in the same ruinous state as when he left.

Recent incomers to Draethen, Rudry, Machen, Bedwas and Trethomas will find it difficult to imagine what life was like from 1939 to 1947 in this relatively quiet, country area. What was it like when the soldiers were 'all about the place all the time' as one young girl remarked? For those who don't remember the war, the bombing raids are equally hard to imagine. The importance and suitability of Ruperra as a training centre is shown by the number of units that were moved in, trained for different aspects of military service and moved on.

The Ministry of Defence chose Ruperra as a Mobile Bakery training headquarters and photographed equipment there for a training manual. One of the soldiers kept his manual, which shows Ruperra Castle unmistakeably in the background, but unacknowledged in the credits because it was a secret location.

A photograph from the Ministry of Defence Mobile Bakery Manual

Many of the soldiers stationed at Ruperra had either had frightening war experiences beforehand at Dunkirk, or went from there to places of death and suffering like Burma or the North African Desert. These experiences have been included in this book because they help to give a complete picture of the fortunes of the 'Ruperra Soldiers' and they set Ruperra in its vital place in the history of the Second World War. The accounts emphasise that those who lived to tell their stories were the lucky ones. Their stories illustrate how war disrupts normal life, and remind us of the sacrifices the conscripted soldiers had to make on our behalf; above all of their cheerfulness in adversity. None of the soldiers elected to describe the really bad things that they endured. Instead they recount the amusing things and the ways that they were able by ingenuity to get the best out of various situations.

One amusing story is described by Barbara Owens whose husband Reg went to Ruperra Castle in the winter of 1939 as a 19 year old in the Territorial Army. There had been a very heavy snowfall and the soldiers were instructed to go up behind the Castle to Craig Ruperra to attack the hillfort.

They were all youngsters and hadn't had much training at that point. They were instructed that some of them were to defend the fort and others to attack it, and they did so with snowballs!

Barbara said

'from the way he told me about it, it looks like they were really enjoying themselves! It was great fun. There'd been quite thick snow and it was quite an exciting exercise!'

Reg Owens visiting the Stable Block in 1995

CHAPTER ONE : WAR COMES TO RUPERRA.

In 1939 the presence of the soldiers at Ruperra and the unfolding events of the Second World War gradually took effect on the life of the local population.

Flo Smillie, *a girl of 19 at the beginning of the war who lived in Twyn Sych in Rudry, married a Ruperra soldier, Scotsman Jim Smillie. She described the presence of the soldiers in Rudry Village.*

"There was dancing in the Castle but my father wouldn't let me go. A lot of the girls from Rudry Village used to go. The soldiers used to come down in the lorries for them and then bring them back in the small hours of the morning.

"All the soldiers at the Castle used to come and go very quickly. I met a Londoner one night and the next day he'd gone. I was waiting for him outside the church and somebody came up and told me. You didn't know when they were going, well, *they* didn't know themselves and perhaps you'd have met them on their last day there. So you couldn't trust them. You'd have been daft to trust them.

"The Indian soldiers were very nice looking, very smart. The girls used to go mad about them. They were really handsome; very pale brown skin and straight as a line. Some of the officers had moustaches and you could have fallen for them although it didn't bother me. It was nice to see them though.

"How I met Jim was like this - I was going up to Greenyard Farm to get milk and these two soldiers were coming down the footpath and I said to myself 'Blinkin' soldiers - I'm fed up with them all about the place all the time,' so I passed them without taking any notice. When I got up to the gate I had to turn round to shut it and they were stuck there looking at me. One shouted up at me 'Shall we come?' I said 'Please yourselves!' When I got into the house I told the housekeeper I wanted to stay there for a bit, because there was a soldier out there and I didn't want to bother. But she said, 'Don't be so soft' and I went out after a bit and he was still there and he came all the way back to the cottage with me and made an appointment to meet me. Soon after he was sent up to Scotland but he kept writing to me and when he had leave he came down and we were married in Rudry Church.

"After Jim and I got married he went straight out to North Africa. He was away four years and when he came back he couldn't settle at first, the war did these things to them, they couldn't help it. You don't know what other people are suffering unless you're going through it yourself. He wouldn't talk about it. He was never even willing to travel after the War; he said he'd travelled enough."

Jim and Flo Smillie

__Rosalie Johnson__, lived in Chatham Street in Machen with her parents.

"The soldiers used to come to the village. When they came on a Sunday, they just couldn't believe that the pubs weren't open! I remember how I actually met Bert. I had my little niece out with me down in the village that day and he just happened to come along and he asked me if the little girl was mine and I said yes. But I soon put him right! My parents took to him straight away. We had fun in those days. The kids today don't get the same fun, do they?

"Bert's unit, only about 20 or 30 men, was billeted in the Castle but we weren't allowed inside. From the summerhouse on the top of Craig Ruperra you could see the Castle with the soldiers around on guard. They seemed to

Bert and Rosalie

11

be the only ones there. I think they were waiting to be posted because I can't remember them doing any baking there and Bert was only at Ruperra for a couple of months."

Ronwy Baumer remembered the war years, as the "good old days. We used to have fun. You don't realise the seriousness of it when you're young do you? We were having a nice time and having a laugh. It was a good life and that was it. I met Frank when a friend of his, who was going out with another Machen girl, invited me to go up to the Castle with them.

"At the beginning of the war they used to have dances in the Castle. A lorry used to come round to take girls there but I couldn't go very often because my mother wouldn't let me. The dances were in the Castle in a proper ballroom.

Tommy Harris of Machen remembers going to only one dance at the Castle. He said "They took us out there, promised us a lift home and then made us walk back. It was a misty old night and we had no coats and we had to walk across the Six o'clock field. This was the easiest way home but it had been ploughed up. The mud came half way up our legs.

"The soldiers used to come to the British Legion club at Machen but they all used to complain about the loneliness and the long walk from the Castle, especially on a winter's night."

Dorothy Jones from Machen knew that there were soldiers at the Castle "because my mother used to do the washing for the officers and the batmen used to bring it down and pick it up. There were always about half a dozen officers there, all through the war and about three batmen used to come with the laundry. We had an old fashioned boiler and a mangle. My father

**Dorothy Jones
today**

died at the beginning of the war when I was sixteen and my younger brother was still at home so my mother had him to keep. The officers paid for the washing themselves. There was a laundry at the Castle for the men but the officers wanted it pressed properly, special shirts and so on."

Eileen Woodward whose father William Greenway had been gamekeeper at the castle before the war, lived at Spout Cottage. She said

"The laundry in Cardiff where the soldiers' washing was taken was bombed out during the war, so they had to find other means, so some bright spark thought that I would do it and so Bill Langstone who was

stationed there used to bring it down. I did it and they never went back to the laundry, they said it was better the way that I was doing it. It was through Bill Langstone being at the castle that we had his family evacuated to us from Birmingham.'

Eileen Woodward in 2006

Byron Evans's father was in the Home Guard. He says "The LDV or Local Defence Volunteers had the huts down at the bottom of Forge Road in Machen which then became the British Legion. The Home Guard used

to go up to Ruperra for exercises and was under canvas in the fields where the deer sheds are. They used to have a field kitchen over there, borrowed from and set up by the soldiers in the Castle. A lot of the people in the Home Guard were in reserved occupations like coalmining or farming so that they were excused military service. A lot had military experience from the 14-18 War.

"They'd camp out for several days with

Byron Evans in 1948

individual tents and big marquees where they'd have their messes and their catering. It was usual for the military commander in the Castle to tap in to the Home Guard for exercises. Sometimes they'd start in Machen, just making a surprise attack on the Castle, which only the commander in the Castle and the Home Guard commander would know about. Those whose fathers were in the Home Guard were allowed occasionally to go up and see the camp. I remember my brother and myself having food with my father in the mess but we never saw any of the attacks.

"It was all very exciting for us. I can remember trains full of Americans going through Machen station. We were all on the bridge shouting down to them and they were shouting back and throwing bars of chocolate and chewing gum up to us. My mother worked for Hartley's fish shop in Machen and the soldiers from the Castle coming from Bedwas Hall cinema would get off the bus right opposite the fish shop by the conker tree. Mrs Hartley would be outside calling them in to make sure they had their free fish and chips to go back to the Castle. They'd go through Forge Lane over the bridge, up to Draethen and through the woods back to the Castle."

*When Byron's wife ,***Tegwen**, *was a little girl of about seven, she went once with the Bedwas Male Voice Choir to Ruperra Castle. She was their elocutionist.* "We went on a coach. We were met outside and taken up the steps and through a big door into the big hallway and a room where there was a big stage. We entertained the soldiers and stayed to eat a meal afterwards. I remember being very much in awe because it was such a beautiful room. There must have been lots of lights and chandeliers there before the War.

Chandelier in the Banqueting Hall

14

"After the concert we sat in a different room at a big oval table. It must have been big because the choir would have been about 30 strong. There were two elocutionists and a soloist, and some of the soldiers were also sitting there. Whether they were the officers or not, I don't know. I remember I didn't have a spoon to stir my tea and one of the soldiers gave me his fountain pen. They made such a fuss of me because I was so young I suppose. I remember standing on the side of the stage, with them cheering and clapping and asking for an encore. I didn't know what to do. There was just this sea of faces.

"I can't remember what I recited there, but in those days it was very sentimental. There was 'Guilty or not guilty' about a little girl who had stolen a loaf of bread and was put in front of a judge, or 'Somebody's Mother' about a little boy helping an old lady across the road. The encores would be humorous though."

Lily Clark lived in Trethomas, a young girl of twenty when the war broke out. On the bus one night she met her husband Sid, who was a baker at the Castle, and they arranged to go to a dance. After the war they went to live in his home in Edmonton.

"Three of us girls who used to go dancing, married fellows from Ruperra. We used to go to the British Legion in Machen or the Grapevine in

Caerphilly or the Workmen's Institute in Trethomas. The War to us was just the soldiers being there. They'd stay at Ruperra between three or four weeks to five or six months I suppose.

"The Castle was burnt down before Sid went there. The men slept in wooden units and they had dancing in a hut. We often used to walk through the forest, 'Out in the wilds,' Sid used to say, with all the forest and everything. It was really beautiful up there.

Lily Clark

15

I'd known Sid about four months before we got married. He knew he wasn't going to be in Ruperra for much longer so he thought we ought to get married before he went. Everybody used to say 'Isn't he handsome!' I was only eight stone four when I got married. We didn't have enough coupons for my wedding dress so all the neighbours in Trethomas chipped in and they helped with the cake and everything."

My first baby was born in 1942, but he was the one that I lost. He was a week overdue and the cord was round his neck. They were short staffed in the hospital with it being the war and that and I didn't have the proper care. My Mum and Dad went to see him, I didn't. They said he was a beautiful baby. Sid sent a telegram, he couldn't come home because he was on the move, you see. He didn't have leave until after everything was all over. His brother and his two sisters came down. I was all right after a while. Tommy was born then two years later, and Siddy thirteen months later.

Sid Church

After Sid came out of the army he still worked in the bakery in London. Then flour got down in his lungs so he worked in engineering till he died. But he *loved* the bakery. He used to make our Christmas cakes and everything. I still miss him. He used to do everything for me. But the boys are very good to me. I see a lot of them. I go down to stay with them some weekends. Then I go to Tommy on Christmas Day and Siddy on Boxing Day! And I go to the club round the corner a lot, we go on trips. I've got some good friends here.

Betty Goodwin lived in New Row in Machen until she married Bert, a Ruperra soldier, in 1944 and went to live with his family in London, returning to Caerphilly fairly recently after he died.

"I met Bert in the Church Hall in Machen where they hold the Machen Remembered meetings now. I think the dance cost one and sixpence. Jimmy Rich and his Band were there. On this particular night I saw a soldier leaning on the mantelpiece there and my friend said 'Go up and ask him to dance.' - it was lady's choice. My Mum had bought me a lovely blue dress with a kind of trellis work on the sleeves and a cowl neck. So I did.

Betty Goodwin

"We used to go down to the Castle over the top of Craig Ruperra from the Draethen and the soldiers would be on guard in the sentry boxes at the gate on the bottom road. The men were billeted in the stables. After meeting him, if Bert was going on duty I'd have to walk back on my own and if not he'd walk back with me.

"Because he was going away, we got married by special licence. I think I'd have broken my heart if he'd gone without marrying me. Bert only had 48 hours leave to get married and he wanted us to go back to London to see his parents. The Newport bus had gone so we went down by the old Post Office in Machen to wait an hour for the next one. Then all of a sudden a little mail van came along, looking like Postman Pat's! They were allowed to give lifts to service men in uniform but Bert said 'There's my wife as well.' In the end the postman agreed to put me in the back covered over with mail bags, in my brown suit and a pill box hat with a veil and feathers on it.

"We stopped to empty mailboxes at Chatham, the White Hart and the Volland, then we went into the Draethen to the box by the Hollybush and

17

then to all the mail boxes all the way to Bassaleg. At Tredegar House I heard the peacocks.

"When we got to Newport Station, Bert went into the NAAFI to get drinks and there were two people from Machen who had caught the later bus and had got there before the mail van. By now it was blackout time, and there were no lights anywhere. The train came in late, also with no lights in it of course and it took ages to get to London.

"We were very happy together. He was still smashing looking in his last photographs not long ago. Meeting him was fate, wasn't it?"

*For the same reason **Dora Hutchings** from Machen has got a soft spot for Ruperra.*

"We were married 43 years. We had a good life together. The first meeting with my husband was the night I had arranged to go to a dance with a girl friend who didn't turn up. Normally I would never go to any function like that without a companion, never walk in on my own. Anyway I thought I'd better just go in and see if she was in the cloakroom, so I paid my money and went in. She wasn't, so I hung about again, afraid to go out of the hall in case I couldn't come back in. I went in to the room and sat on one of the benches. By this time I felt really embarrassed and so self-conscious because only I was there besides the two ladies on the table taking the money. I sat and sat and kept telling myself that I was going to get up and go home but I couldn't even find the courage to do that.

Dora's wedding

18

Then this soldier came in. He walked across the floor towards me and as I stood up I said 'I'm not very good' 'He said, 'You'll be alright!' We danced every dance."

Dora Hutchings

Terry Everson

Terry Everson was a teenaged girl when the soldiers came to Ruperra. She remembered them walking from Ruperra Castle into Machen village.

"I can remember the Indian Army soldiers well. Living in Machen, we had never seen coloured people and so when the Indian soldiers came into the village they were really something to look at! They were Indians, real Indians and they wore turbans!

Roy Hawkins

Roy Hawkins had lived in an estate cottage along the Ruperra drive since 1927 when he was a little boy of three. In the early part of the war he was working for Bill Anstey at Ruperra Home Farm

"the soldiers used to come down past the farm on route march. There'd be about 50 or 60 of them and it would sound lovely, their boots crunching on the gravel, all in step and whistling as they were going, as happy as Larry.

"Since the way to the Castle from Home Farm was closed, we'd have to go in to get the pigswill through the main gate, past the sentry, to the bin by the door between the Castle and the Bothy where the cooking ranges were. There were always soldiers around, going back and fore. At one time there was a bugler there who would blow the bugle at teatime and at 10 o'clock at night. It was a tune like 'Come to the cookhouse door, boys!' and it sounded lovely! I suppose the acoustics were right."

Colin Anstey at Rhyd y Gwern Farm was accused by Captain Brown from the Castle of being a collaborator!

"We had a field full of couch and stubble. It was lovely autumn weather, so we raked up all this dry stuff into little piles and set fire to it. Of course a bit of wind came up when it got dark and the damn stuff, which was still smouldering, showed up as lights all over the field.

Nancy and Colin Anstey

"The captain came up to the house. He said 'You ought to be locked up. We'll all be killed.' I hadn't even thought about it, you know! We were just farming! We had to go down in the middle of the night and put these blasted fires out."

Colin's wife Nancy remembered that they had officers from the castle and their wives staying at the farmhouse.

"The wives stayed on with us after D Day. Of course we were always busy on the farm, milking and that and we had to leave them to look after themselves. They helped us where they could. They had a sitting room and two bedrooms but they could come and do their cooking out in the kitchen, which for me took a bit of getting used to. But they were all very good payers and one of the women knitted a whole cot suit for Beryl, our daughter, in a beautiful pink."

*Doris **Oram**, living in The Row in Draethen, remembers her husband talking to the soldiers marching down past her house.*

The Row in Draethen

"In those days we used to sleep with the window of our bedroom downstairs open. Some nights we'd be in bed and we'd hear something coming in through the window! The soldiers would have thrown in a cauliflower that they'd pulled up from Anstey's in Rhyd y Gwern. Imagine the mess, but it was lovely to have it. A cauliflower would last for days when it was just us two My husband used to feel so guilty when he talked to Mr Anstey but he couldn't say, could he."

*Eight year old **Bernard Spooner** from Machen saw the bread being distributed from the bakery units at the Castle to the Searchlight Batteries around the area.*

Bernard Spooner
Aged 8

"They just threw the loaves into the back of small lorries. We used to hope and pray that one of the loaves would fall off the back of the lorry as they were coming down through Draethen village. We didn't have white bread. Only the Army had white bread. We had 'national' bread, wholemeal, which was probably much better for us but we used to smell these lorries coming with fresh bread on them and our mouths used to water. If there was a good soldier on the back he'd accidentally drop one out and there'd be a scuffle for it."

Ethel Ackland *remembered that when she and her husband Bill and their family were living in Parkwall Cottage along the Ruperra Drive in 1942,*

"We had an awful job to move because the soldiers were always having target practice when we wanted to go out along the drive to the main road. They used to shoot down on the flat by the deer sheds and they'd be shooting into the hill. It was all right when they'd stick to the target but sometimes the bullets would whizz over and drop down as far as Cwm Leyshon. It was terrifying. We were right in the firing line there. We couldn't even go in the garden in the day. We had a job to get the children to school. We used to bring them to the corner of the lane and they'd meet the other children and all go in a gang, so I went down to see the officer, who said 'the soldiers training is much more important than your children's schooling.'"

Winifred, *Ethel and Bill's 10 year old daughter when she got home from school would see British soldiers* "dug in trenches inside the park, right the way from Ruperra Park Lodge (there was no fence there then) right across to the cherry trees by the footpath in John Wells' wood and down to the avenue of oaks. We kids all used to go over to the soldiers, collect their jerry cans, fill them from a tap in the corner of the outhouse at the Orams' cottage and take them back. Every night they'd give us money. That's why we used to do it."

Ruperra Park Lodge in the 1980s

22

CHAPTER TWO : THE FIRST SOLDIERS AT THE CASTLE

The first soldiers to be billeted at Ruperra Castle were from a unit of the Cardiff Territorial Army.

Gordon Crooke *from Fairwater who had made out that he was 17 so as to join up, said*

"We were the first soldiers in to the Castle and the only ones there at that time. It had been totally emptied and workmen were taking out the last bits of whatever had been in there. We could see little bits of the wonderful staircase which was now boxed in with white timber and looked so out of place. We had no beds. Our pillows were our gas masks."

Gordon Crooke as a young soldier.

Before being stationed at the Castle, the unit had been hastily got together to form the Royal Corps of Signals when the outbreak of war seemed imminent. ***Jack Senior*** *from Cardiff described the process*:

"The Drill Hall, a decrepit old place, was next to the GPO in Cardiff where the new stadium is now. We used the shelter of the old Arms Park stands to drill and that's all we did to train for war! We marched up and down in civilian clothes, with one rifle between ten of us and we were the T A!

"Then a couple of days after the outbreak of war, I told my mother that we were definitely moving and didn't know when we'd be back, so she made me some Welsh cakes as if to say 'see you in 12 months time.' The Western Welsh buses arrived and took us to Druidstone House in St Mellons. We were back home at 4 o'clock!

"At first we organised our unit so well that every day we did a little bit of drill in the morning and by 12 o'clock were getting dressed up and

cleaned up and by 1 o'clock we were down on the main road thumbing a lift home
.

"All of a sudden, 'A' Company will proceed to Ruperra Castle.' Nobody had heard of it. When we arrived it was a bit awesome because there was nothing there but the Castle and the transport area. There was nothing inside the Castle either, no bunks, no beds. We were given 'bedding space' and were up on the third floor. The second floor was occupied by a number of officers and on the ground floor were the offices and the Officers' Mess. The kitchens were also on the ground floor and the food was pretty good. The amount of work that had gone on to protect the Castle impressed us. Planks had been fastened down on to the steps and stairs and on some of the floors of the main rooms on the ground floor. Nobody thought of the fire risks.

"There were light bulbs in the ceiling but nothing happened when you switched on. It took the transport section about 3 days to strip down the generator which was found in one of the outbuildings and put it back together again. Lights emerged, dim and yellow. So the order went out that the upper floor would use the lights between 8 and 9 in the evening and the second floor, where the officers' bedrooms were, could use it between 9 and 11, so as not to blow up the generator."

The Generator Block to the left of the Stable Block taken before the war

Cyril Cozens a TA man from Portsmouth came to Ruperra from Druidstone House where conditions had been bad. At Ruperra however

Cyril Cozens in 1999

"we slept within four walls and in a fairly large room with a good roof, in the Stable block. Someone had been in before and put in some quickly manufactured two tiered bunks. I don't remember actually going inside the Castle at all. The Administration and the Regimental Officers were in the Castle. It was all very makeshift at the time with straw palliasses and blankets. Washing and shaving was a cold water job. Baths were organised at Druidstone and I imagine it must have been the same at Ruperra. A certain number of people went every morning to Cardiff to the public baths. It was my job to see that half a dozen trucks would start every day, which they never did because there weren't even half a dozen trucks with good batteries. So you got one going and then towed the rest to start them.'

Jack Senior noted that "nothing had been done for the comfort of the men in terms of latrines. We were being inspected every now and then by groups of officers who appeared to have a little bit of influence. and soon a gang of men arrived to dig a great big trench. They put up a bit of a shelter over the top of it and then some engineers arrived and put down a fantastic pumping system to pump chemicals along the latrine. The man in charge was given instructions to dilute the chemical at a ratio of 2 pints per 40 gallons of water, but

Jack Senior in 2001

he poured it down neat and the place was well occupied at the time. Quite a number of people had to go to hospital as they had left their seats rather quickly. It was a beautiful building too. It was about 30 yards from the castle."

Cyril Cozens remembered the overcoat problem. "At Ruperra round about Christmas 1939, we received the first intake of the Militia boys to train them for all sorts of communication work. It was cold and these conscripts had to do their share of standing guard and there weren't enough army overcoats to go round. So all the TA. lads had to hand in their army overcoats to keep the Militia warm, who, since they hadn't asked to join up, had to be treated properly. We old regulars were still in the original mountain dress with old leather bandoliers, ammunition pouches, and breeches for the Dispatch Riders and so on. So I can remember being 'properly dressed' in a black and white overcoat from the 50 Shilling Tailors in Cardiff worn over my pre-war uniform. The Army had just bought up anything they could that was an overcoat.

Jack Senior added that "somebody had had a brilliant idea – they served a notice on the Fifty Shilling Tailors in Cardiff ! No. 1 Company had blue Melton overcoats with velvet collars because we were the elite! No. 2 Company which was not so good as us had brown ones and No. 3 Company who were the real roughs and toughs, had everything that was left. You can just imagine what the first Church parade looked like. And this silly existence carried on for quite a while and then all of a sudden a different presence arrived. Five foot three, a little bristly moustache, he came from a regular army unit. And that chap's job was to turn us into soldiers and he did!

Stan Lavery and Roy Reeves were dispatch riders from Barry

"We slept in the stables and kept our bikes in the courtyard. They didn't have enough motorbikes so at first you had to use your own motorcycle. Then the Army started taking a gang of us on a lorry to the BSA works in Birmingham and we used to pick up BSAs or Nortons. These were proper

26

Army cycles then so we could leave our own at home. I remember one Saturday coming back from leave and running all the way back to the castle thinking that if I can get in early and check in, then I can get out again and go home without

Part of the Signals Unit, Roy and Stan on the left but not at Ruperra.

anyone noticing. And I was the only one of those on leave that got back in the Castle. It was full of German measles and once I got in I couldn't get out again. All those that took their time to come back weren't let in and were sent back home.

"It's funny how things are. When we were at Ruperra Castle we became Catholics (I was Methodist really). We found out that on a Sunday morning as there was no church service for the Catholics in Ruperra, they had to go to Cardiff. When it started there was about one wagonload of Catholics going to Cardiff and when it finished there were about 3. We'd drop off the back of the wagon by Cardiff Castle and go home to Barry. The Army twigged it in the end because the number of Catholics was increasing so much."

CHAPTER THREE : THE 38th ROYAL CORPS OF SIGNALS

(Previous page) Members of the 38th Royal Corps of Signals at Ruperra in 1940 before leaving for France (Cyril Cozens third from the right)

In the Royal Corps of Signals, most men were army 'tradesmen', that is wireless and telephone operators, dispatch riders, linemen, electricians and so on, who received extra training and therefore extra pay.

***Cyril Cozens**, remembered the early days.* "When I was at Ruperra, everything to do with radio was still very primitive but we were responsible for keeping the lines of communication open. At the beginning, messages were written out and given to a DR *(dispatch rider)* to deliver

Cyril Cozens in the centre.

***Jack Senior** describes the equipment that eventually arrived to turn the TA unit into the Royal Corps of Signals.*

"Although the telephones and the Morse Code machines were from 1918, we were gradually turned into a Signals unit and we were given training rooms on the second floor of the Castle."

To put their training into practice, they went up into the woods behind the Castle. "The radio sets were very big and heavy. It was a real struggle for one man on his own, but on the other hand they were really awkward for two to carry and there were big batteries with them as well. We

Jack Senior wearing his bandolier (see above)

29

went all the way up and did everything according to the book but didn't receive or send a message all day. Back at camp we found that the exercise for running the lines up to the telephones hadn't worked either. It had been an absolute fiasco. Some of the equipment had been in storage since 1918 and had never been checked over".

Dispatch riders (Cyril Cozens in the centre)

Gordon Crooke also was a dispatch rider.

"The Stable Block was our workshop where we had to maintain everything. We had been trained before the War to repair anything that went wrong. The motorbikes and equipment were put in the stables and the radios were set up and we started our normal work within 24 hours. I was running all over the country, back and 'fore on the motorbike

Gordon Crook in the Stable Block in 2000

30

throughout the winter of '39 and into the summer of 1940.

"We had very little free time. As dispatch riders we had a roster. There were about thirty or forty of us and you could see by looking at the roster when your turn was imminent. But also you'd know when you could have an hour off and go and have a kip. Sometimes you'd have perhaps three or four hours off. Other times you'd come in off a run and they'd be waiting for you to go back out."

*Serious training work was now being carried out. **Cyril Cozens** worked on training men for vehicle repair.*

"Officer Jock Simmons was in charge of the Transport and Dispatch Riders at Druidstone and Ruperra and I was his right hand man. There were about 10 of us, two fitters and eight chaps helping. I had already served my time and my father was an instructor in the RAF on aero engines. The other trainer/fitter, Cliff Stone, was an ex Bedford apprentice. There'd be about 50 to 100 men coming in at a time to be trained for signals work. The vehicles were those needed to pick up supplies of food, clothing and bedding for the surrounding camps but there were none available in 1939 and so we had to build them. The Army was buying in all kinds of old cars from the 1930s. Anything over 20 HP, including Sunbeams, American Buicks, Packards, were brought in to Ruperra from all over the country. We'd go up to Birmingham or Wolverhampton and bring a convoy of them back. Then the bodies were cut through behind the driving seat and a box body put on to the back to make it into van. These vans carried radio sets for communications as well as troops and were kept in and around Ruperra Castle - by the houses, the stables and by the engine house. I remember using the smith's forge to straighten up an axle when someone had been in a crash. We were not necessarily under cover - we'd work on the vans where they were - all around the grounds."

*
Jack Senior loaded his van up one day with fairly modern (1920) radio equipment* "'and I jumped in the front with the driver, because I wasn't an operator then, and we left Ruperra at quite a quick turn of speed, towards

31

the road. After a while I said to the driver, 'The blokes in the back are quiet, aren't they'. He said 'Yes, they must be hanging on like grim death.' So we stopped and had a look and there was nobody there. No tail boards had been put on the back of the trucks, so when the driver had put his foot on the accelerator the whole lot of them had just shot out. They were still on the parade ground when we got back".

Lorries, on the other hand, were often hired by the week. **Cyril Cozens** *says that only when they totally broke down could they go back to their owners.* "However, if they could be patched up, they *were* patched up. And they *were* old vehicles. I think our oldest was a 1928 coal lorry. Not that that was terribly old in 1940 but these were primitive vehicles of the 20's and they weren't brilliant when they were brand new.

"I remember one Saturday night in the early days of the War, when people were still going to the cinema in the black out and the streets were crowded, a Ford van had broken down in Queen Street. I had rung Captain Simmonds to say that the van had a broken crown wheel and pinion and needed a new back axle. His answer was 'Well repair it!' I pointed out that the Ford works were shut at 10 o'clock on a Saturday night but he said 'Well go and wake them up. Find where the manager lives and get whatever it is you want and fetch the vehicle back. I'll send you down some rations.' So he sent down another van with some food and some blankets. 'If you finish it in the middle of the night,' he said 'have a kip in the back of the van.' I shall never forget it. We found some 40 gallon oil drums and we stood the van up on them to repair it. In the end I couldn't bring it right in to the Castle because there was a lorry broken down in the middle of the drive. They said 'We thought we'd let you find out for yourselves that you've got to repair that one as well.'

"I remember coming back from the valleys one day with an ambulance on a hire agreement that we'd take it back to the owner for repair. At the time we had some terrible old wrecks that we couldn't get rid of unless they were absolutely clapped out. We had to keep using them. So when this ambulance broke down I used a dreadful old Morris coal cart to tow it back up the valleys. The Captain said to me 'You'll never make it in that Morris.' And I said 'I hope I won't. I think I'll get there but I hope I won't get back. Then we can get rid of the Morris as well.' Anyway, coming back I broke the connecting rod and blew the crank case out of it just within sight of Ruperra Lodge gate! Done it! Victory!"

*In one of the units who were supposed to be trained at Ruperra by Cyril Cozens and his mates was **Arthur Lewis** from Newport. But most of the training had been done and there was nobody who knew what to do with these conscripts. He remembered his first night at Ruperra Castle very well.*

"It was the most cataclysmic day of my life. Hundreds of men aged 25 were ordered under the Conscription Act to catch a train from Newport at 10 am to Monmouth where we gathered in a field at stake posts allocated to different regiments. At 7 pm after an embarrassing medical and having been given nothing to eat all day, the 30 of us that were left, all at the Royal Signals stake, were taken off in cars impressed for the army and converted into light vans. We arrived at Ruperra Castle in the gathering gloom where no arrangements had been made for this unexpected party. We found out later that most of the trained men had already been drafted out and no one was expecting any more trainees.

"We were given a roll call and taken to a store room where we were given a canvas bag to fill with straw and a blanket which we had to sign for. Then we were allocated sleeping spaces in the Banqueting Hall and at last given a mug of cocoa and some doorstep sandwiches. I lay on the floor looking up at the minstrel gallery in the dim light (oil hurricane lamps I think). The sense of foreboding that I felt then still recurs when I think about that day. I had little sleep that night. I was devastated.

"Next day the transformation from 'Mr' to Signalman 2362012 took place. Fortunately the weather was kind and we erected bell tents on the grass in front of the Castle and slept there for our remaining stay. A few days later we heard about the evacuation from Dunkirk and all leave was cancelled."

The 38th Welsh Divisional Signals were then split up and Arthur was transferred into the 102 Yeomanry, going to North Africa with the First

Army. He was involved in some heavy fighting in Algeria and then Monte Casino in Italy.

On one occasion the whole regiment was cut off for 12 hours by a German Goering Division of parachutists. Under attack at the same time by Messerscmitts, the British soldiers did not know that there was only a very small number of Germans cutting them off. A British officer was able to take a small 25 lb shell gun up a hill from where the whole situation could be seen. The gun was fired and the regiment was freed.

Arthur recalled the propaganda leaflets that the Germans dropped on the First Army, urging surrender: on one side a picture of a blonde woman with the caption 'Gentlemen prefer blondes', on the other, a British Tommy on crutches with 'Blondes prefer gentlemen without crutches.'

Gorden Crooke *describes the departure of the 38th Royal Corps of Signals in June 1940. after the dispatch riders had formed a light car section.*

"One day twenty beautiful new little Austins rolled up and twenty of the dispatch riders were trained to drive them and were sent to the Middle East. They went from Ruperra Castle and not one of them returned. They were friends of mine and I made enquiries after the war, but not one of them had survived.

"Those of us that were left at Ruperra were transferred into the 48th Div Signals Group and sent to India, Burma and Malaya until the end of the war. We just

Gordon Crook in 2001

missed getting home for Christmas by one day in 1945. By then all that was left from my TA unit was myself, three Cardiff boys and one Caerphilly boy. Out of the two hundred men of my Signals unit going into Burma, only twenty nine came out at Rangoon. I found this out at a reunion in London after the war. I had gone into the room expecting to find it crowded. There were just twenty nine people scattered about talking quietly. It was a shock."

34

Jack Senior went to the Middle East and was taken prisoner in Italy after surviving Tobruk and Alamein. When Italy surrendered he went to a Prisoner of War Camp in Germany. When Germany surrendered he managed to escape the advancing Russians and met up with some Americans, who he found sitting on a jeep in the middle of a road. He flung his arms around the big black captain's neck and kissed him! He and his two friends then had the difficult task of persuading the Americans that they really were British soldiers. The officer used this foolproof method.

Jack Senior today

"He sent for one of the unit who grilled us as follows. "When you come out of the General Station in Cardiff and turn right, what's the first pub you come to?' 'It's not a pub Sir, it's the Great Western Hotel' He said 'You've scored one. Now, you keep on down that road, what do you run into if you don't turn off?' We thought 'What the hell do you run into down St Mary Street?' I said 'You run into the Castle.' He said 'Strike Two!' Then he said 'When you come down that street and you turn to the right what street would you be in?' I said 'Queen Street.' 'What's in Queen Street?' I said 'A load of shops.' And he said 'You're right. They're in, Captain, they're in.' So the captain gets a bottle, knocks the top off and says, 'Have a drink!' We did and the three of us passed out on the floor. We hadn't had any whisky or anything like that for a long, long time and there was the shock and everything. One tot out of a bottle was enough."

Cyril Cousins pictured here in 1999 was drafted to Japan at the end of the War as part of the leading repair / recovery crew for the Japanese beachhead. Although he was due to be demobbed, there were only about 5 replacements for trained staff left in the whole of the Central Mediterranean Forces and his replacement in Japan didn't come until April 1946. There was nothing he could do about it!

CHAPTER FOUR : THE ROYAL ARMY SERVICE CORPS

As the Signals moved out of Ruperra in June 1940, the Bakers moved in. The bakery units were very quickly trained and moved on in a couple of months. Some of the soldiers had been bakers before the War started and were then trained to instruct the others. Some came to Ruperra after Dunkirk, however, and just stayed there for a while to recover while their units were being reformed.

A bakery unit on the east porch of Ruperra Castle

*The first time **Norman Baxter** from Gillingham arrived at Ruperra was after returning from Dunkirk. He had been a baker before the war in the RASC in the Army Bakery in Chatham.*

"In France, although the Germans were advancing, we had kept on baking bread. Then one day the order came to drop everything and evacuate. After a week however they sent us back. Everything was just as we'd left it. Dough and everything all over the place and the Germans hadn't got there. But then we really had to go. I think we were only just in front of the Germans. I came out of Cherbourg on a Belgian ferry. As we were leaving we could see all the smoke where we'd set our oil tanks on fire.

Norman Baxter in 1999

"When we got off the boat we were put on to a train for Hereford, where we slept on the race course in the open, and the following morning we went to Ruperra. We slept in the Castle on the floor - no mattresses, just two blankets and that was it. We ate in the Castle too. We didn't have to go outside for anything. As far as I remember, our unit had its own cooks. We didn't do any baking there since we'd had to leave all our equipment in France. We used to

have to get up in the early hours of the morning, dress in full kit, proceed to where coaches were parked and sit in them for a couple of hours in case the Germans invaded. Then we'd have to go back into the Castle and were kept occupied with drills and so on.

"We were only there until the 7th July 1940 and I have a clear memory of being lined up ready to move out and seeing the Second Field Bakery moving in. Those early bakeries had quite a lot of men in them, three or four hundred I suppose."

John Rogers, a baker from Deal in Kent, met his wife, then Betty Cage of Machen, when he was a soldier at Ruperra. John had gone over to France in 1940.

"The 2nd and 3rd Field Bakeries were one unit at first and went into France together, with the Brigade of Guards Amoured Division. It was in the evening and scorching hot as we went out into the Channel. This was the invasion.

John and Betty's wedding

John's subsequent experience in France supports Norman Baxter's. At two o'clock one morning they were called out of the cotton mill where they were baking and issued with 30 rounds of ammunition for their rifles because the Panzer tanks were coming.

"We left everything behind. Dough in the troughs, bread in the ovens, we just had to run and get down in a ditch either side of the road with our rifles and 6 bayonets. One of our men accidentally squeezed the trigger and the chap in front got it in the back and was sent home in a box. Nice fellow too. We then had to walk miles to find a train to take us away. We came back eventually - the dough was all blown up all over the floor and we had to clean it all up and start again. Then in a week we had to move again - this time for real."

John's unit was then called on parade one morning and divided up. Left half to number 2 Field Bakery and Right half to number 3 Field Bakery. In the evacuation from Dunkirk many from number 2 were on the Canberra, the ship where the bomb went down the funnel. John's life was saved because he was in the right hand half.

John's unit came to Ruperra straight from Dunkirk and they didn't do any baking there. He says,

"When we were at Ruperra, my billet was in the apple drying room on top of the electricity generating room. We NCOs, being away from the main unit, had bedside lights. I had a two tiered bunk and, as the one above was empty, I fixed a wire to come down so that after lights out I could switch on and lie in bed reading.

One night - as I was guard commander - I found some screw bulbs in the pump house, stood on the table by my bed and put one in. Flash! My hand went blue and the whole Castle went into darkness. There were panic stations. They wanted to know what had happened but I didn't admit to what I'd done. After that there weren't any more bedside lamps!

John returned to Ruperra in 1943 after the Castle had been burnt down and slept under canvas in the grounds. He says

'There was a big tump at Ruperra where the favourite horses were buried. We slept on the ground on palliasses with a ground sheet under us and a couple of blankets over us. I remembered then that in France I had slept on a door to stop the water soaking up from the ground.

This time we brought our mobile bakery equipment to Ruperra which became the number 1 training base for all bakery units. Men were being recalled from the Middle East and from various parts of England. We baked under marquees and the ovens stayed on the trailers with canvas over. We did the baking out in the field under canvas.

For the purpose of taking the photographs for the Ministry of Defence we had to take the equipment out into the open.

The illustrations for the Ministry of Defence instruction manuals for Mobile Bakeries were taken in the grounds of Ruperra Castle. The booklet included detailed technical instructions and information as well as pictures of the canvas accommodated equipment. It seems then that the photographs were taken after the fire although the castle itself in the picture shown here, looks in a pre- fire condition.

A Mobile Bakery- canvas accommodated

A Mobile Bakery – Working Layout of Trailers

A Mobile Bakery – Feeding the Divider

We trained a whole American unit at Ruperra. They had brought their own equipment as far as Ireland, but when they saw how compact and efficient ours was, they left their stuff there and came to us for training. I was attached to them for a while. They were sleeping under canvas too but they had their own quarters.

Being with the Americans was an interesting experience. I was walking through the field one morning with our RSM, an Irish bloke called Paddy, and an American Captain. An American private came up, just strolled across to the Captain, didn't salute and asked if he could borrow some money. Our Paddy's face went a deep red, he looked as though he was going to explode on the spot but he couldn't interfere.

There was plenty of food with the American unit. Big bowls of sugar and 'Help yourself!' packets of Camels, but there was one problem. The Americans had their own food plates which had three divisions. We only had two so when we ate with the Americans we got our dinner in one division and our sweet and gravy together in another. And chicken - we got sick of the sight of chicken!"

At the end of the war, John did some very valuable work in France clearing the airstrips of mines.

"We arrived at Courcelles in France after D-Day. The fact that we were bakers didn't mean a thing and because our equipment hadn't arrived over - it hadn't been given priority - and since they don't believe in you being idle a minute, they gave a group of us a three ton lorry, a length of chain, and a sergeant. We had a roving commission to go anywhere we wanted. We had to fix our chain to the poles that the retreating army had put in the airfields to stop our planes from landing. We had to pull these poles up so that the Airforce could use them as airstrips.

But you never knew until you pulled one up whether it was booby-trapped or not. That's how we lost our sergeant. We had to pull them up and hope for the best. I mean it wasn't as if we were Royal Engineers - we were bakers.

"Before we did that the fighter planes that came over had go all the way back from Caen to the East coast of England to refuel. With these airstrips cleared they could refuel and be back again within the hour. And Monty thanked us personally for what we had done because it was so important and we got priority leave to come home. It was the only time we got thanked for anything in the Army. So we got sent home even before the people who were at D-Day. But the explosions affected my hearing, and I've got compensation for 50% loss.

George Archer, a widower who lived in Machen, was one of the bakery trainers. He had joined up into the RASC when he was twenty.

"Ruperra Castle had been burnt down before I went there. We slept and lived in little wooden huts but the surroundings were beautiful. Everywhere you looked there were lovely woods and green trees.

"We'd be up at 3 o'clock, get washed and dressed and stand by our beds for inspection. Even the studs on our boots had to be very very clean. In the tents were troughs, 3 by 8 feet, and the ingredients would be all ready weighed out for us in buckets by the side. They put lard in the bread in those days and it made it very filling. You had to mix, knead and cut, mix, knead and cut, throwing it each time into the next trough.

The lads would watch what I was doing and try to copy me and I would go round to see that they were doing it right. You had to knead two loaves at the same time. Some of them would say they'd never worked so hard in their lives.

"Then the loaves would finally be put on a rack, wheeled to the oven and gently slid in. Each oven held 60 loaves and there were three of them. The mouth part was under the canvas but the rest was out in the open. When the loaves were baked they were cooled off, stacked in tea chests and sent in lorries to all the camps around.

A mobile bakery – Setting the oven

"We'd finish work at two in the afternoon and then our time was our own. We'd walk through the woods down to Draethen village and have tea in Mrs Britain's. Some one said to me "You want to watch it walking through those woods behind the Hollybush. There's a ghost there called the White Lady." You know every time I went up and down there I used to look for this white ghost. We'd always be two or three soldiers together. I'd never have walked through those woods on my own.

"From Draethen we'd walk through the fields on a path already made with all the soldiers walking on it previously and go down to Machen.

They were nice times. Everyone was very, very good to us. That was when I met my wife. She was from Machen but I didn't have much time there after we were married. Two days later I was away to Italy until the end of the War."

John Geddes *wasn't at Ruperra very long*

"but I have pleasant memories of it. The Commanding Officer must have been Bashford. I remember doing a second class baking test there but it was just theory, we didn't actually bake there. I can remember the iron gates there with a guard on them. I think we slept on bunk beds in a stone building. Any wood that was there was dark and blended in well with the stone. The lectures were in a hut and there was a community room there as well. It was quiet in our sleeping quarters and it was good for getting on with our notes from the lectures. By the time I came into the army you were separated out into your trade. At the beginning they didn't ask, they just trained people

"It was a very nice warm summer when I was at Ruperra. We used to walk over the fields to Machen. Someone invited us to tea one day. My mother used to do the same at home in Lossiemouth when the soldiers were there."

"I was in Egypt for the main part of my army time. We had the bakery machine generators on permanent bases in Egypt most of the time. However with the mobile bakery you could if necessary actually be

packed up and moved in minutes. We have also made bread when there were no ovens available, by digging up the open ground to make an oven

"There were a lot of British soldiers out in Egypt after January 1946. I was up near the Aswan dam and it was so hot that the bread used to go bad because it couldn't cool down properly. People realised later on that it was the wrong sort of bread for that area. The Arabs never ate our sort of bread. They ate naan bread.

"We actually came home on leave from Egypt. That was an innovative thing at the time round

John Geddes in Egypt

about January or February 1947. It was the worst winter in living memory. I was cold all the time I was home and I was never warm till I got back again!

"My regiment was in the Z reserve and so after the war I could be called up at any time for several years. I'd only been out 3 years when the Korean War broke out and I had to go for a few weeks to a camp with a bakery unit.

Iory Pearce from Chirk was already a baker before he joined up in 1944 at the age of 18. After being in Glasgow for six weeks he went down to Ruperra while his unit was being formed.

"Only our unit was there and then after six to eight weeks we were moved on. We never baked a loaf there. We used to buy the bread in the local shop. We just used to hang around, go to the local villages and to Newport for a day out. We used to go drinking, but we'd always come back here for the dances because the beer was cheaper in the NAAFI.

"There was a bit of a square in front of the Castle to the right of it with a nissen hut. I can remember a bloke coming in to the nissen hut and saying he'd play the piano if somebody'd play the drums and that was how we had the dances at night. The nissen hut was used as a dance hall, an eating place, the mess and the NAAFI shop. Our quarters were on the left of the Castle. The Castle was already burnt down. Every morning, we'd come from our quarters to the square to fall in and be checked.

"I never remember doing anything at Ruperra except hang around. In fact that was my life in the Army hanging around and doing nothing but travel. I actually only made bread in Portadown and Hongkong. I went to Barry, Ruperra, Penarth, Barry again, through the night to Stranraer, to Laugharne, to Portadown, which was a lovely place and lovely people, back to Barry Island, Ruperra and Caerphilly Drill Hall (where I met my brother who was in the Royal Welsh Fusiliers.) Then India, Ceylon, the South China Sea and Japan. There were about 40 in my unit being sent around the world. They didn't seem to know what to do with us. It's a lovely journey to India and three weeks on the boat. But I did it four times!

"To us, going there for the first time in '44/'45, having hardly been out of Chirk, India was a completely strange place. When we arrived, there were riots in Bombay and Kalian. Later on, it seemed a very nice place. We saw quite a few snakes which was a new experience to us. When I was travelling on the train to Allahabad I got dysentery. The conditions on our train were terrible. They were trucks not carriages and there were just holes in the floor for toilets. The journey took twelve days. I suppose it wasn't too bad since only six of us got dysentery out of the forty on the train. I was cured after five days in hospital. I lost a lot of weight though. You'd have really funny things wrong with you, ringworm, rashes, boils and bites and you'd be covered with purple gentian violet.

"In India we used to go on twenty mile route marches about 7 o'clock at night when the sun was going down and we'd often we'd see camel trains, hundreds of camels in a row and you'd be walking along past them.

"On the boats we slept below deck. I couldn't sleep in a hammock, so I used to sleep on a dining table with the hammock swinging above me. Very strange and very, very hot. In the day you could sit around and site see, like through the Suez Canal.

"Ceylon was a beautiful place, then Chittagong in Bangladesh was very unusual. The Malacca Straits is the most beautiful part of the world you'd ever wish to see. The sea there was dead calm. But we ran into a typhoon in the South China Sea!

"As we were going in between the two mountains that come down into Hong Kong harbour, -which is very beautiful - some lads noticed a periscope in the water - and this was after the Armistice had been signed in Singapore. It turned out to be a British two-man submarine, a midget, but I remember thinking 'I hope I don't die here after all this.

"While I was at Hong Kong I went up the Yangtze to Shanghai and from there to Kure in Japan where I met my brother again, then to the Philippines and home for two weeks leave. I was on the boat for 5 weeks.

46

That was the year of the bad snow, '47 so I couldn't get back without an extra week's leave! Japan was very nice. My brother took me to see Nagasaki after the bomb. There was nothing there except one concrete building left standing!

"I don't know how I managed to find my brother in Caerphilly, Yamaha and Kure amongst all the hundreds and thousands of soldiers in the Far East, but I did. At last I got demobbed and I hadn't done anything anywhere except for baking bread in Portadown and Hong Kong!

"When I was in hospital here at home not so long ago having a small operation, some of them asked me to tell them about the Far East so I told them about the snakes and that. The following morning the Ward Sister told me they were throwing me out! All the men in the ward had been seeing snakes dancing on their beds all night! I had slept like a log of course. I had to be careful what I said about my experiences in the Far East after that!"

Roy Dukes from Edgware, enlisted first in the Royal Army Medical Corps in April 1940. In 1944, after two years with the Catering Corps, he was posted to the paratroopers although he said he wouldn't have volunteered for that. Because he had done a catering course, he was in charge of the cooking for the 80 men in the platoon. He said,

Roy Dukes in 1999

"If there wasn't a fire to cook on out on manoeuvres we would use oil and water. You'd get a brick and put a metal pin down. As one part of water and one of oil splashed down, there would be enough fire made to cook on. Other times, once you'd done the cooking you'd put the food into hay boxes, half cooked and sealed down, where it would go on cooking. Then on manoeuvres, out would come the boxes with the food all ready to dish out

"I don't think I cooked at Ruperra. I was just billeted in the Castle for a while at the beginning of 1941. The Castle itself was a big place. Inside were the Sergeants' Mess, the Officers' Mess and the canteen and many different rooms. We'd have to go up a lot of stairs to get to the room where we slept on the floor on palliasses, and looking out, you'd see the mountains.

"From Ruperra I went to Holland, when it was occupied by the Germans. About 30 of us would do a 'recce'. The civilians would direct us to the safe houses where we could hide, get and also pass on information.

"Towards the end of the war, we were in Wiemar where we joined up with the Russians. We got on well with them. We were on the move all the time, fighting. At night, you got down in the shelter of trees somewhere, put up your bivouac, had a sleep and then were on the move again. You'd always carry your haversack rations with you, things that would last for weeks. If you happened to be by a stream, you could have a wash, but only then.

"The Germans were retreating all the time. Once, I had to get one of them to pull his trousers down to make sure he was safe - or rather that I was safe! - because I didn't know what weapons he was hiding in his trousers. I felt it was a wicked thing to do but you can't take any chances when you're at war. Once you had them in a prisoner of war camp you could be nice to them. You didn't have to be nasty all the time once you'd captured them.

"When we went into Germany, everybody was looting. We still didn't know when the war was going to end but we were having to check people's houses to make sure that there were no soldiers left. Many a house I've gone in to where the husband and wife were dead and the house looted. They'd take what they wanted, move on and find another house with something else a bit better. Then they'd sling the first lot away. You just imagine going into somebody's house when they're not there or even dead. You could take all their silver or whatever you liked. Otherwise somebody else would, or it would get bombed and buried.

"Often when searching a house you'd find a cellar full of Germans civilians hoping they wouldn't be found. You could either shoot them or let them get on with it. I never had the heart to shoot them. I know it was war but they were civilians and so you've got to give and take haven't you.

"We did a lot of fighting in the Gaza Strip. We arrived there in March 1946. Often when we would go into a town in Palestine all the shops there would be open but as soon as they saw the red berets, down would come the shutters and you wouldn't see a soul. They were scared of the Paratroopers."

CHAPTER FIVE : THE 307 SEARCHLIGHT REGIMENT

The Tyne Electrical Engineers Searchlight Regiment which came to Ruperra had also been at Dunkirk as part of the British Expeditionary Force. Once again the soldiers' stories show how unprepared for war Britain was in 1939 and how much of a lottery survival was.

Wartime photograph of a searchlight in action…in daylight!

After landing back in Britain, the 307 Searchlight Regiment was sent to different parts of the country, setting up searchlight stations as they went, and eventually arriving at Ruperra, which became their HQ.

For Lance Robinson and Cecil Hogg, *the early days of the War had been frightening. When the War started,* **Lance** *was in the Merchant Navy and half way between Vancouver and Melbourne.*

"I was sailing over the international dateline so I was in the war before it started! We discharged the cargo of timber in Melbourne, where we had a gun put aboard the ship and went to gunnery school. Then we were put in the Army and given a boiler suit, a cap and a pair of dungarees while waiting for a uniform. Wearing these I was sent to France with the BEF (British Expeditionary Force) and if I hadn't gone to the gunnery school in Australia I wouldn't even have known how to hold a rifle.

Cecil continued

"We were too late to be picked up at Dunkirk and made a run for it, breaking into cottages and getting what food we could, through the fields from Honfleur to a little port by the side of St.Malo. One of the lads saw a boat, the Black Prince, a Thames pleasure steamer, and we ran down and got on it.

After landing at Ramsgate they marched us into the goods yard, where the Women's Voluntary Aid Service gave us Woodbines and apples and shoved us aboard a train for Taunton. The next morning at Taunton Manor Barracks we were stood there, hungry and dirty, and saw the notices. 'The BEF shall not wash here, The BEF will not use these toilets, The BEF will not do this and so on. Some of the lads had to dig trenches for us to use as toilets. We had to sleep on the floor of a big gym with blankets and then they came round with that brown stew stuff on a tin plate. It was shocking. They didn't want us there because it was a training place for young soldiers and they didn't want them to hear our bad experiences. There were so many soldiers coming back into the country from Dunkirk that they didn't know what to do with them. They gave us 48 hours leave to go home but as soon as we got to Tyneside it was time to go back.

In November 1941 the regiment had orders to move to South Wales, the new Battery Headquarters being Ruperra Castle. Cecil, as a supply driver, was in the advance party.

A typical Army supply lorry

He said

"Ruperra would have been an ideal headquarters. We had a lot of transport you see, wagons and things needed to be stored. There were all those stables and storage places at Ruperra. The whole unit was about 500 men with 24 sites and my job was going around all these sites and seeing to their supplies of oil and diesel, any breakdowns, generator repairs. Unfortunately we were only a couple of weeks in Ruperra before it took fire so we had to find new headquarters quickly to keep up communications with our detachments.

"I remember having to pick up a load of fire bombs in Cheltenham for Ruperra. I wonder if they're still there! They gave us a strict route which kept us away from all cafes and traffic and that. We were given half a dozen petrol cans full of water and we had to keep stopping and wetting the bombs to stop them exploding. When I got to Ruperra, the Sergeant Major came out and said 'Come on now dump them in that bloody lake, keep them out the road! *(Cecil said to me 'It's dry now is it? Oh well they must have found them then.')*

Lance *remembers the fatigues every morning.*

"They lined everybody up in the yard and those that had permanent jobs could fall out. Those that were left were designated cleaning work, toilets, this and that. Right at the top of the Castle was one special room, the toilet, where we could go for a rest. There were about ten 'nettie' seats as we Geordies call them. We all used to sit there and the Sergeant Major used to shout 'There's about 100 bloody rooms in this Castle, why do you have to all be in that one!'

"As far as I remember we used to eat in a big room with trestle tables in it, which might have been the kitchen, somewhere at the bottom of the castle. And I can remember clearly one night, going with a mate to the British Legion in Machen. There was an old boy about 90 there, an Eisteddfod gold medallist, a really good singer. I shall never forget him. In the nights you used to be able to hear the lads singing on their way back along the road from the Club. There was one night on our way to Machen we were lost in the forest and didn't even get as far as the Hollybush!'"

*Another member of the Tyne Electrical Engineers was **Andy Newton**. He had lived in South Shields before the War, where he joined the Territorial Army.*

"In 1939 most of the TA soldiers were only 19 or 20 years old but a few were much older and had been in the 1914-18 War. You'd notice when you were doing PT that they couldn't keep up! People used to say to me

'What did you want to join the Territorials for?' One reason was that my cousin was there and in fairness also I think it's a good outlet for a youngster in peacetime. Anyway if I hadn't, I'd have been called up when the war broke out and probably been in an infantry unit. As it was I didn't see any hand-to-hand fighting and I had a lot to be thankful for.

"When the unit went over to France as part of the B.E.F., we heard the messages from Lord

Andy Newton in 1999

Haw Haw, broadcasting to try and upset the troops. 'Don't bother about meeting up with your friends because we've sunk them on the way across.' Naturally we were very concerned because most of us had relatives from the same unit going over to Le Havre on different boats. Of course when we got there, we met up with them.

"We did have a bit of bombing at Le Havre. The unit couldn't be evacuated as a whole from Le Havre, because the searchlight sites were so scattered. So the men had to make their own way to the coast. On one site the engineers were ordered to blow up the trees around the site before leaving. This straightaway put back all the mess that we had been clearing up in the house we had been billeted in.

"During the evacuation it was unbelievable how many wasteful orders there were from the Sergeants. For example we were ordered to destroy our remaining lorries so that they wouldn't fall into German hands. But they could have been used to take men to the coast and then destroyed. My lorry that I refused to blow up, took a crowd of us to Le Havre and was then useful for generating power in the house that we were living in while waiting for a ship. When we left, all our remaining lorries, and even new bren gun carriers, were pushed over the cliffs.

"Then, after leaving on a ship, we were sent back to France to man the barricades at Rennes with 1 rifle between 4 men. Then, when France capitulated, we boarded a hospital ship at St Malo but had to throw all our ammunition over board because ammunition wasn't allowed on a hospital ship!

"When we eventually came back from France my unit was stationed at Rhyl for a few weeks. There's a beautiful little church near the camp in Rhyl with about 40 or 50 graves of Canadians killed in the last days of the 1914/18 War. It seems they were billeted there and had been promised a ship to take them home. There had been a riot in the camp and our own troops had shot and killed them. What a terrible thing to have gone right through a war, to be back on friendly soil and then to be killed.

"After Rhyl we went to Hanley Swan and then Ruperra. I was in the headquarters unit which used to supply the searchlight sites with rations and service the lorries and Lister generators. A report would be given to Cecil Hogg (*see above*) every morning about the state of fuel on the sites so that he could deliver it.

"There was a monthly lorry inspection, called a 406, a sort of MOT to see that they were serviceable. One of the sites we used to service was right on the top of a mountain at Mamhilad. We had to get the RAOC to get the generator up there. Whenever we went there to see to a lorry, we had to stop by a house at the bottom of the hill to phone the site and a chap used to come down on a donkey. I can picture him now sat astride the donkey singing, 'I've got spurs that jingle jangle jingle!' He had an old straw hat on and he really looked the part. We used to fasten all the tools on the donkey and they would be carried all the way up. We'd have to follow walking. It was quite a climb.

"Invariably Cecil's lorry broke down outside a pub. Whenever he broke down someone would ask 'Is he outside a pub?' But of course, in fairness, he'd use the pub as a reference because all the signposts had been taken down. On one occasion he was found on three wheels right outside a pub on the Gloucester to Bristol road! The load of stuff he had on had kept the lorry upright but the front stub axle had actually snapped.

"When I went to Ruperra I'd been used to living in South Shields. We had some beautiful parks up there but coming to a place like Ruperra with no houses around was really outstanding for us. We felt like royalty living in a place like that. When we arrived there was a bit of a mess around the grounds. The Castle itself wasn't too bad but the outside areas where the soldiers had been walking were trampled and there was rubbish lying about. It was pretty depressing when we first went there. The area facing west had been used as a latrine.

"My first impression though was what a lovely place it was right in the middle of the country. The gardens were very nice because at the time there were a lot of trees in flower. The inside of the Castle was out of this world, beautiful. In the main hall they had a beautiful marble fireplace, which in fact was still intact after the fire. It's nice to see photographs of how it used to look - it brings back memories. In the billet where I was,

Andy Newton in the engine house in 2000

right at the top, there were wide south facing windowsills and we used to lie flat-out there in the sun. On a clear day you had a beautiful view to the other side of the Channel.

"To the left of the stable block was the engine house where there were the two big horizontal steam engines to drive the power generators. They had big long piston shafts, and big fly wheels, beautiful things, and I actually saw them running. We weren't really allowed in there unless we happened to see the caretaker, Tom Pembridge going in to look after them. Also in there was a water pump and motor to drive it, which went down into a deep well. Tom Pembridge used to give it a run every so often. He used to keep all those engines beautifully polished and clean.

"There were coal fires lit in the kitchens which were down below ground level, massive places. We used to go in the kitchen occasionally to try and scrounge a bit of extra. I think we had our meals in the basement. We were outside most of the time of course. I think the toilets were outside.

"After the fire, we went to Druidstone and from there to St.Michaels, Llandaff and the Transport Section was moved down to Llandaff Fields. Then on a night off, I met a girl who worked in the local laundry. While I was talking to her, her pal came up. I was attracted to her straightaway. Each time I went out with the first one I would see this other girl (who eventually became my wife) and would try to make a date with her. Of course she would refuse because I was dating her friend. I used to meet this girl on the old iron bridge in Llandaff and one night she didn't turn up. I'd seen Grace, my wife to be, on the bus stop so I went over to her and persuaded her that I wasn't going to see the other girl again. It was St. Patrick's night when I first took her out. She was always late meeting me and I think I knew every blooming rivet on that bridge - I'd counted them so many times. We got married in Llandaff Cathedral because my wife's little church had been bombed. So had the Cathedral, but we got married in the Lady Chapel. As we came out the boys were lining the path and they had put a load of prams there! And Grace and I were there wheeling them out of the way. It was a good laugh..... Memories!

"I hadn't been back to Ruperra for some time. I clearly remember a massive walnut tree opposite the main entrance. After the War I took the wife and daughter up there a few times and we had quite a few walnuts. The place was open then, there were no restrictions and we used to get beautiful walnuts. I should imagine it's been chopped down by now and sold for timber.

"When my wife was ill she didn't feel like going anywhere, but then I bought a little car and we went out every day round all the areas we used

56

to go to when we were courting, but we never got back up to Ruperra Castle. We thought about it many times but we never got back."

*Another member of the 307 Battery, was **Ray Neville** from Newport.*

"My unit joined the Tyne Electrical Engineers in 1940 just before we went to France. I was on the concentrator, keeping in telephone contact with each of the sites. Then we were kitted out and sent to France as part of the BEF and we had our searchlight sites around Le Havre.

"I remember the German bombers going over Le Havre and writing home to tell my parents how the ack ack fire was way off target and a long way behind the planes. Eventually when I got home on leave my father told me that all that information had been blacked out. I didn't think when I wrote it that it might be censored. We were only young lads, twenty years old or so.

"For the evacuation from Le Havre, where it was all chaos, they took names out of a hat. The unlucky ones had to remain behind on the roadblocks for a period, to hold the Germans back if they could. The lucky ones, and that included me, were able to get on a Bedford lorry and get to St. Malo. When we got to the quay, there was just one boat there and they were pulling up the gangplanks. We ran along and just managed to get on.

Ray Neville

"On the lorry at Le Havre, all we had had for food were tins of corned beef and army 'dog' biscuits, which were square and hard like cement no matter what you did to them. Then, on the boat, we found a load of tins of Libby's condensed milk. Of course once you were half way through a tin you felt sick.

"We landed at Southampton and were sent to Taunton to be kitted out. Then to Stonehouse, then Hanley Swan and then to Ruperra, which at first was the Searchlight HQ from where sites such as Ponthir and Bulmore Road were organised. When I was on the switchboard, one officer used to say, 'Get me Palmers Green 0875' That was his young lady in London. We'd put him through but I think he knew that we'd all be listening to the conversation.

"I remember the very elegant wooden panels all around the walls of the rooms and the big towers there. We ate on the ground floor on army trestle type tables. One chap did stand up and complain about the food and it improved afterwards. Normally when the orderly officer of the day asked for complaints, no one would say anything. Happy Days!

"We slept on the first floor in a big room, about 9 or 10 of us on palliasses. You'd put your ground sheet down first and then this straw-filled palliasse. You'd have blankets and a straw filled pillow case. The straw used to go flat in no time and was very uncomfortable. They'd change it every so often.

I can recall that if you had anything to eat in the night and you left it by the side of the bed the rats would eat it while you slept! They didn't come out while we were awake, you wouldn't know they were there until the first time you'd leave some food by your bed. Rough days! I'd never been used to it but there was nothing else for it, you had to *get* used to it.

"After the units were formed, the men went out from Ruperra to the various searchlight sites in a 15 cwt lorry. I was the telephonist on our site. Nine people ran each site. Of these, one doubled as the cook and there were portable ovens. Every day a 15 cwt lorry, the 'ration wagon' from HQ, would bring the rations for the 9 of us to the site. Our accommodation was in bell tents and I don't recall any heating. There had been no heating in the castle but on the sites that winter of 1941 it was so cold that the bell tents were covered by a marquee. The only place you could have a warm was in the cookhouse round the old stove. For toilets we had to dig a trench for ourselves with a pole to sit on.

"The Searchlight sites were organised like this. Number 1 was the NCOIC (officer in charge of the site). Numbers 2 and 3 were spotters scanning the skies for enemy aircraft. Number 4 operated the long arm of the searchlight controlling the up and down movement. Number 5, my

58

A searchlight spotter

position, used to change the carbons in the lamp and we were taught how to 'expose,' and then 'dowse', when instructed. Numbers 6, 7 and 8 were on the sound locator estimating and pinpointing the direction of the enemy aircraft from the noise that they made. Number 9 drove and operated the lorry which carried the Lister electric generator for the searchlight. The Lister, which could be moved around, generated 150 volts and the smaller lamp took 75 amps so that was a fair old whack of power.

"Most of the searchlight sites were around Caerleon. I was at Bulmore Road. They had guns up at the top of Christchurch at Belmont. We were down in the valley, illuminating any enemy aircraft that came over with a huge 120 centimetre lamp searchlight.

"I remember my stay at Ruperra well. I was living in Newport, so whenever I came back from leave I'd get off the bus at Lower Machen and walk to the little village of Draethen with its row of little cottages, and then go up behind the Hollybush and through the woods to the Castle.

Ray Neville today

*Another member of the same regiment, **Frank McClary** was about 27 when he was called up from the building trade in Penzance in the second year of the war.*

"I went straight in to the 307 Searchlights Battery. With 3 other batteries they made up the 37th Regiment. Apart from another Cornish boy from Marazion they were mostly Geordies in the regiment. It was a job to understand what they were saying. You didn't get to know many other people in the regiment because you were out on the sites all the time

"There were four batteries to the 307 Seachlight Regiment, four troops to the battery and six sites to one troop.

Frank McClary in 2000

The Regimental HQ was in Llandaff and I only once or twice came in contact with it. Messages were relayed from the troop HQ to the battery HQ and a lorry would come round with the supplies. The Troop HQ was on one of the sites and was called Charlie 1 in the troop that I was attached to. On the site which was the troop HQ there would be an officer. On the other sites there would be a sergeant in charge or a bombardier or perhaps a lance bombardier.

There were 2 sorts of searchlights. There were the small ones that you could transport on a lorry and the other bigger one that you towed behind the lorry. The small one had caterpillar wheels and drove on to the lorry. Then you had a cab behind the driver to carry the searchlight crew. Sometimes you'd put 3 searchlights together so as to have a greater concentration of light. I was at Tewkesbury in the Cotswolds when the German bombers were

90 cm Searchlight with caterpillar tracks going over in droves night after night to bomb Coventry. They were going right over us. The

60

searchlights would pick out the bombers for the fighters to go and attack them. It was a fighter aircraft area there and so there weren't any guns. Otherwise if you had had guns you'd be blowing up your own planes.

"The big searchlights measured 150 centimetres and the small ones 90. That was the distance between the positive carbon and the reflecting mirror. There was a big concave mirror inside the searchlight. The positive and negative carbide had to be touching. When you'd put the knife switch down they would fall apart and form the flame which was then reflected off the mirror and up into the sky. The only servicing that was needed was that the carbons had to be changed because they burned.

"The sites were usually a few miles apart and scattered all round. On my site I was number 4 most of the time. I was in charge of moving the long

arm of the light up and down as necessary. But if the searchlight operator was away you'd have to be ready to operate the actual searchlight.

One of the men on the site would be the cook. You were supposed to have a sentry on guard all the time.

Number 4 – A long arm operator

"After the Cotswolds we were in Abergavenny, with the Battery HQ in Usk, then at Hanley Swan near Malvern. That was our battery fort and we were in the rear party, getting ready to be moved to the Battery headquarters at Ruperra Castle, where we would be organised and made ready to go out on site. The Tyne Electrical Engineers were already stationed there. While we were clearing up at Hanley Swan we had word that Ruperra Castle had burnt down. So we had to pack up quickly and come down with the advance party, staying at Ruperra for one night and going on to Cardiff, to St Michael's, Llandaff City. So in the end it was at St Michael's and not Ruperra where we got ready before moving out on to the sites.

"At Ruperra, we just moved in one night and then out again in the morning. We slept in the stable block overnight, in bunk beds. There was a cook on site in Ruperra. The Castle was burnt down; it was a ruin. They said that there wasn't enough water there to put the fire out. We walked inside and had a look. It was quite a mess. I can remember the beautiful big staircase going up; the treads were still there.

"At first on the sites we were in bell tents. It was only towards the end of the war that we went into huts. At Leckwith it was so muddy that you had to put gumboots on to get out of the field. You'd leave them by the gate then, and put your ordinary boots on. We slept on tent boards. Sometimes there'd be two layers of bricks underneath them to keep them out of the water and mud. Compared with that it was luxury sleeping in the Stable Block at Ruperra.

I was stationed down in Nash in Newport one Christmas. We were having Christmas dinner in a marquee and we had benches to sit on. We had gumboots, on with the mud half way up to our knees, and the bench would start to sink backwards into the mud and we'd have to get up and pull the seat up. Of course the next minute we'd be falling forwards on to the table. Christmas dinner!

"On the sites we had to entertain ourselves - dominoes and that. If you wanted to be out at night you would need 24 hours leave. Otherwise trips to town were mostly in the daytime because we had to be in before sunset to be on duty. When I had leave, I went home a couple of times but it was a long way by train all round Gloucester to get to Penzance. There was one officer who would give you two 24 hour passes, one to follow the other. He wasn't allowed to give a 48 hour one, so he would leave the second destination blank for you to fill in yourself. Some of the officers were very good to us.

Frank McClary and searchlight comrades pictured at Briwnant

"I was at Briwnant on Caerphilly Mountain. The site was in a field near the Black Cock Pub and there's a little quarry in the woods there with a path coming up from Taffs Well. While I was there, Craig, the War Minister, came up and inspected it. Everybody up there had to brush a bit of paint on, so that if you touched anything, you got paint on you. We all had new overalls brought up for us in a van which waited there while the inspection was going on. Then as soon as the visit was over the overalls were taken off and put in the van, which had to beat the War Minister to the next site he was going to inspect.

"When I was in Cardiff I got quinsy pretty badly and they sent me up to Maendiff Court at Abergavenny for convalescence. There, we used to see them taking Rudolf Hess for a walk in the afternoons. There'd be 2 officers, one either side of him and 4 stick guards, 2 in front and 2 behind, and they'd go up behind the Little Skyrrid and around the lanes for a walk. One afternoon I was going out down along a quite narrow path and just one officer was coming up taking Hess out for a walk. I had to go between them because I had to salute the officer. Hess knew this of course and so he had to step to one side. I was closer to him than I am to you and he tripped a bit and nearly fell down. He looked different then from what he finished up like on the television. He'd gone to nothing then. He had grey serge trousers on and a sports coat. He was a fine looking bloke. He was kept in an annexe in a little lodge and he had guards there all the time.

"My wife died 13 years ago in the afternoon of the 15th December. That was the date I moved out of Ruperra Castle in 1941. Then when I went up to the Cemetery here in Penzance to see her grave, the number on it was 307, the number of the Searchlight Regiment.

Some of the local veterans visit their old billet in September 2001. From left to right – Frank Baumer, Gordon Crook, Stan Lavery, Roy Reeves, and Andy Newton.

Lower Machen, Draethen and Coed Ruperra in 1954. Ruperra Castle is in the top right hand corner. RAF Aerial Photo Crown Copyright.

CHAPTER SIX : THE GREAT BOMBING RAID JANUARY 1941

Many people thought that having soldiers at the Castle was going to make the area a target for German bombers. The real target, however, was not the Castle but the Rogerstone Aluminium works where parts for British aeroplanes were being made. However there was still some confusion, particularly in the big raid early in 1941.

Vernon Morgan *from Rogerstone explained that they were making aluminium strip and sheet at the works for aircraft production.* "Reclaimed aluminium was brought in from crashed aircraft and re-used, but they never actually assembled any aircraft there. It would still be an attractive target for the Germans, so a smoke screen was put around the whole area, the main roads and the country lanes as well. The method was to fill big canisters (like very large dustbins with a cowl on the top) with crude oil and set fire to them when a raid was expected. They gave off volumes of dreadful smoke. It depended on the direction of the wind which ones they would light so that the works would give the impression of a large lake. But you couldn't go to bed at night and leave your windows open. The smoke was dreadful. Sometimes the canisters would flare up and that would cause a bit of consternation because *they* became a target then. You would have expected the Germans to have worked out eventually that the smoke screen was there for a purpose, but the Works were never hit.

"Until two years before the war, the 'Rodgy' Works as they were called had been the Guest Keen and Nettlefords steelworks. Now there were about 10,000 people employed there, both locals and from the valleys. A lot of women worked there, more than men, who were away in the war."

Herbie Spring from the Draethen believed that Coed Ruperra being laid out as it was with different blocks of fir trees looked like camouflage from the air and was being mistaken for the Rogerstone Works.

"This place used to get hammered with incendiary bombs and we children used to pick up the fins off the incendiary bombs and take them home. I can remember larger bomb cases which my uncle would empty for us to use as money boxes. They stood about a foot or more high, and the top, which he would unscrew, used to fit over the tapered part."

Herbie Spring in 1948

Ethel Ackland described the big raid in January 1941 when she was living at Park Wall Cottage along the Ruperra drive. Her husband Bill, who was an ARP warden, had gone with Jim Moses from the Cynant farm to an agricultural meeting at White Cross.

Parkwall Cottage in the 1950s

"And although they could see all the light over here from the bombs, they couldn't use the headlights on the van to get home quickly because of the blackout. By this time Mr and Mrs Blackburn from the Preserve had collected all their insurance papers and valuables together and had crawled all the way up across the park in between the incendiaries coming down. When it was dark they'd crawl a bit and make a bit of progress. If we'd had a bomb on our house that night there'd have been a lot more people there than normal. The children were on the mattress under the table where I would put them

67

every night. And then Mrs Hawkins and Roy came and joined us. Then Bill and Mr Blackburn, who was a warden as well, went out and left us. The incendiary bombs were dropping all over the place. They narrowly missed our house. The ceilings came down in the outside buildings. It was terrifying. The Ack Ack guns were firing over our way at aeroplanes over the Channel so we had the shells as well and the mobile guns were around the roads."

Enid Thomas' family at Cwm Leyshon Cottage could see Park Wall Cottage all lit up with incendiaries.

Cwm Leyshon Cottage

"My brother Elwyn said 'We're in the front line tonight. Big bombs are going to follow now. The best for you is to get under the stairs'. Suddenly someone knocked at our door and asked to come in. It was Mrs Oram, who lived across the field from us. She looked around at us and seeing we weren't very bothered asked whether we knew what was going on. We could hear the big guns along the Channel. My sister Madge and myself and Mrs Oram got under the stairs. Dad said he couldn't breathe under there (he had silicosis) so he got under the kitchen table. We never thought that if we'd had a direct hit, what would have killed us was the 130 lb of jam on a shelf under the stairs. We had gone right under the shelf and Mrs Oram was praying 'Oh God, Save my Arthur!' Then another bomb would go off and she'd say 'Oh God, Save my Ernie!'

"There were often air raid warnings" *remembered* **Roy Hawkins** "and although incendiaries would fall there would be no big bombs dropped. This particular night was different. The shells were exploding from the anti-aircraft guns and the shrapnel was whizzing through the air. Then the

68

bombs started to fall and every time you heard this screaming noise, you thought that it was meant for you. It was very frightening. When the incendiaries dropped, it was like a wind rushing. The nearest bomb to the Castle was the one by the Home Farm entrance by the side of the Michaelstone road."

Bernard Spooner *already knew the difference between the sounds of the British aircraft and the German.* "If they had been up to Birmingham or Coventry on a bombing raid and were coming back using the moonlight on the River Severn as their navigation aid, they would dump their bombs anywhere along the route. That's why we used to fear moonlit nights. I remember being hit out of bed one morning - well I don't remember it since I didn't wake up. My mother told me that she'd put me back into bed. A landmine had dropped in the river 50 yards away.

"She used to take me up on to Ruperra Park on a Sunday afternoon to watch the dog fights over the Bristol Channel and planes being shot down into the Bristol Channel. It was wonderful when the spitfires were winning! Of course the Bristol Channel was very busy, there was Avonmouth, Bristol, Cardiff, Swansea, Newport and until the end of the war with no radar for guidance, at night time they just relied on moonlight."

Dennis Penny *was eight years old in 1941 and living in Ruperra Park Lodge. His father was Police Sergeant Penny who as a policeman was part of the ARP team for the area. As soon as the siren went, Sergeant Penny would have to go out on duty to the field above Ty Gawla where he, Bert Strading, Bill Ackland and Jim Moses could see across the Channel and keep watch on what was happening, and where the bombs were dropping.*

"I used to hate the sound of the Caerphilly siren, warning us that there was going to be a raid.

**Sergeant Penny
on the Ruperra Drive**

Positioned between Cardiff and Newport we were bound to have stray bombs, and the siren frightened me to death. Incendiaries would be dropped first to mark out and light up the targets for the bombs.

Dennis Penny today

"The night of the big bombing raid I was in the house with my mother, my two sisters and my aunty. At first my elder sister had taken us outside to look at a house down in the Cwm surrounded by a circle of incendiary bombs. But then it turned into a nightmare. I was absolutely terrified. We were all cwched up under the stone slab in the pantry. Three bombs were dropped but my father heard only two explosions. One was by the side of our house, fortunately in a ditch but although the house had thick wooden doors, the blast blew them straight off. No one knew where the second one was, but the third dropped on rocky ground by the old Mill and took its roof off.

"My Aunty Cissie discovered the hole where the second bomb was, a delayed action bomb, thirty foot below ground on the footpath between the Mill and the Ruperra Drive. The bomb disposal people took a fortnight to dig down the thirty feet, clear the area and detonate it. A couple of us boys went down afterwards to see the huge hole and picked up massive pieces of shrapnel."

As local residents go about their daily business, racing to work in Cardiff or walking and riding in a leisurely way around the countryside, it is very difficult to imagine the terror that bombing raids engender. The Rudry and Draethen one lasted just one night and that was bad enough.

CHAPTER SEVEN : THE ROYAL ARMY MEDICAL CORPS

Frank Baumer volunteered in 1940 at the age of 20 and was taken into the Field Ambulance Corps and sent for training at Ruperra. Most of his 152 Field Ambulance Unit were Londoners from Fleet near Aldershot They came to Ruperra Castle by lorry and entered the grounds by the Lodge on the Michaelstone road. When they got out of the lorry and saw all the trees around, somebody said, 'What a bleedin' dump!'

The 181st Regiment of the Royal Army Medical Corps were there already, and billeted in the Castle. The 152 which became absorbed into the 181 lived outside in bell tents in the Castle grounds. There was also a detachment of Royal Army Service Corps drivers for the ambulances which were kept at the back of the Castle. Frank said

"We had a marquee where we used to eat, right by the porch and steps of the Castle door on the east side. We used to go into a big room upstairs in the Castle to play Housey Housey and table games. There were flagstone floors where we came in on the ground floor facing the staircase. I'd been working as a french polisher from the age of 15 and I particularly took notice of the doors in the Castle. They were lovely doors, a light coloured teak about two inches thick.

The Hollybush today

"All round the Castle there were beautiful rhododendron bushes and paths like lawns in the woods. The lovely grass drive up to the summer house was about twelve foot wide. Then between the path and the bushes on the verge of the bank, there were daffodils and narcissi. "We used to cut down through the woods to the Hollybush where Mr Rae, the keeper, lived. It wasn't a pub then. Mrs Lloyd and Mrs Britain had little tea gardens in the Row in Draethen where we soldiers used to go. Before I was introduced to my wife, we used to go to

Bedwas Hall on a Friday night on the 'passion wagon' from Ruperra, which dropped us off and picked us up. My future mother-in-law, who was on the British Legion committee, used to do sandwiches for the soldiers every night in the Machen Rugby Club.

"We had a regiment of the Indian Army attached to us, looking after the mules and camped on a field the other side of the Castle. When we went over there, they'd call out, 'Johnny come and have a cup of 'chai.' To us, their tea was terribly sweet because they were allowed more sugar than us. They used to bring their mules up to the gravel on the east side of the castle.

Our training included putting large medical panniers on either side of the mules. This used to frighten me to death, because they would kick out as we were trying to strap the panniers down. The Indians used to hold the mules steady, but you'd often see them dragged along the floor for about 30 yards if the mule bolted. But they wouldn't let go, they were very brave. Then they'd take them back to their field to unload them again.

An Indian Officer

"There was an Indian officer, all dressed up in white shammy gloves, who used to go round the mules, smooth them and look on his glove for any dust. If he found any, he'd play hell with the soldiers. He used to go on horseback on the route marches while the Indian soldiers used to walk, leading the mules, and we all walked as well. When we went on manoeuvres, we'd go up through the woods to the Hollybush and on past Machen railway station, ending up in Brecon, which would take about two weeks.

"Two of us would walk behind each Indian soldier with his loaded mule, carrying a stretcher with a blanket inside.

We would walk about 20 miles a day. You'd end up putting the handles of the stretcher between the webbing on your uniform because your hands would be all blistered. I wore out a new pair of Army boots one fortnight while I was away. People came out to give us water but the sergeants wouldn't let us take any. We were carrying water bottles on our side, a full pack on our backs and a gas mask in front plus a steel helmet. It was exhausting but that was the training. They must have been training us for a mountainous region, but in fact we were sent to the Desert.

"On manoeuvres, we slept in the fields with our gas capes wrapped around us. We went right up in the mountains. There were marvellous views although I didn't appreciate them at the time. The mules stampeded through our field one night. I jumped up from the ground and managed to get to one side just in time as a mule came leaping over me. Of course the Indians had to catch them then, but they were good at it, fair play. I should think there were about 50 horses - it seemed more the night they stampeded.

"Then an airborne division was brought in to Ruperra to train to use gliders and half the unit volunteered to go in it. I didn't fancy it. Anyway, we were given a Pegasus on our shoulders and a red beret and after that the airborne ones went from the castle. The rest of us went to Talycoed. That was where we heard that the Castle had burnt down.

"Then we were sent abroad and joined the UK 14th Field Ambulance Unit in the Gaza strip. We ended up at Alamein. There it seemed that for a long time nothing happened. Then one night General Montgomery came to talk to us. It was very quiet. 'Be prepared,' he said, 'tonight we're going to hit them for six.' Around 10 o'clock everything opened up and you could feel the desert shaking.

"Our unit was right there behind the battle line to receive all the casualties. Over our 3 ton vehicle we had a canvas sheet and tents for the medical unit. The stretcher bearers would bring the casualties a short distance to us in ambulances and we used to see to them, give them a cup of tea - they loved a cup of tea, it won the war I should say - and then the medical officers would take over. That was where we got our experience of proper war. When I knew the battle was going to start, I said to the boys 'I can't stand the sight of blood, it makes me feel faint' but the funny

Frank Baumer's photographs of El Alamein : The lorry and medical unit are indicated by a flag on the right hand side of the top picture

thing was, once it started and you saw them all coming in, you just got on with it. Then they were sent by ambulance down the line to Cairo or Alexandria, to the Army medical units there and the Queen Alexandra nurses.

"One time, as I was bandaging a chap's leg and talking to him to take his mind off things, I asked him where he came from because I could hear he was Welsh. 'Oh', he said 'It's a little place, you wouldn't know it.' So I said, 'I don't know, it's possible, where is it?' He said 'It's a little place called Machen.' I said 'Do you know Jim the Post ?' 'Jim the Post!' he said and I can see his face now. 'I'm Fred Buckley, I live in 3 Club Row.'"

Jim Bell in 2007

*Another man, **Jim Bell** started his army career as a regular at Fleet, Aldershot. He came to Ruperra when war broke out for extra training as an ambulance man.*

"I joined up in '38. I was only 17 then, little did I know the war was going to break out, but that was what I wanted to do. I was posted to Midfield General Hospital and in February 1941 they sent just four of us down to Newport. Nobody knew or wanted to know who we were or where we were supposed to be. We were turned away from the Stow Hill barracks, and Barrack Hill and the Defence Volunteers Unit down the Dock – although of course in fairness we weren't volunteers.

Eventually the four of them, two privates and two corporals were sent to Alexandra Road School where a kind lady gave them a meal and put them up. The headquarters of the 152 Field Ambulance 32 Corps was then set up as part of the 8th Army. There Jim met his wife, a Newport girl and after being posted to Paisley and Inverarray he ended up at Ruperra Castle. Although he was overjoyed to be coming home when he went to Ruperra Castle, they were only there for a few months.

*They used the main entrance on the Cefn Mably road and as all the
ambulances and vehicles used to go out that way they could easily get a
lift.*

'Once when I'd had my tetanus jab I was off duty and tried to get a lift in
one of the ambulances home to Newport, but there was a sergeant major
sitting in the front! He sent me back!

*Bill remembered that if they wanted a walk they would go down through
Draethen where a Mrs Lewis kept a café.*

"My mate brought his wife down from Birmingham and they stopped with
Mr Lewis for the weekend since he had a week end pass. When I went
back there after the war, I got talking to a chap who turned out to be Mr
Lewis and he remembered me coming in the café. In the Machen Working
Men's club- the steward there was a lady called Mrs Cann. When I go to
Newport on the bus now it brings back memories.

"At Ruperra we were billeted in one of the towers at the back with eight
or ten of us all the way round that room. I remember the stairs and the
Hall – there was a mess room there and rooms for the officers and the
clerical staff – we were all upstairs; we were three companies about fifty
in each company, officers and NCOs. The Service Corps - RASC - were
there the same time with us with a major to each company and two
captains, a lieutenant, one regimental sergeant major and other sergeants
in each company and three corporals and lance corps and privates and a
colonel in charge of the lot

"The officers were in one wing of the castle and us in the other. The big
hall was the dining room for us men and they'd serve us there from the
basement cookhouse. I don't know where the officers' mess was. The
food was good. They used the ambulances to go to Abergavenny to the
depot to get the rations.

"After Ruperra we went back up to Scotland and then to North Africa
through Sicily and Italy to Austria and we were there three years. While
we were up in Scotland, I volunteered to be an orderly because I thought,

if we're going abroad now, you've got the ambulance and you've got somewhere to sleep. So the ambulance driver took the first aid course and then I took the driving course so I could drive if he got wounded and if I was wounded he could do the first aid.

"When we first went over to North Africa in '42, they had cardboard tanks put on the road side so that the Germans would think we had tanks. We were in a little farmhouse with a camouflage net over the trees. We'd got our heads down this one night and suddenly noticed how quiet it was. We found our regiment had gone, retreated back and the Germans were advancing. If we hadn't woken up then, they'd have taken us prisoner. On another occasion, we heard what we thought were some locals calling out us and didn't know what to do, but they were calling because they had an American pilot who had baled out and was wounded, so we had to take him back to our first aid post. They could have handed him over to either side and luckily enough for him we were there.

"One time in the general hospital in Austria – Claggenfort - there was an Italian interpreter there with me. He and his parents had come to live in Blackpool before the war, he'd come back to Italy and of course they'd kept him there and conscripted him into the Italian Army to fight with the Germans. When we were half way up through Italy, the Italians had packed in and they had very little food so I said come and have food with us because we were then having American rations which were marvellous compared with the British. The British used to have sausages made of sawdust with bacon and beans; we had biscuits that we had to soak in the tea before we could eat them. If there was an A on the box you'd know it would be better than that and the Yanks had bread too – I don't know where they got it from - and chocolates and sweets.

"Anyway the Italian said to me "will you write home for me because my people don't know where I am so I wrote a letter to his parents in Blackpool telling them that he was alright.

"Monte Casino in Italy was called the 'mad mile' because the ambulances couldn't get up there so we had jeeps and the jeeps only had angle iron and four wounded stretchers. The stretcher bearers had to carry the wounded down from the top of the mount to the jeeps. The Germans could see us and they could have shot us - all we had was the Red Cross flag on the jeep.

"But then we went further up to the Sangro and the last river was the Po and that was near the end of May or June in 1945. The Americans were there then with their anti personnel bombs and they were bombing us by mistake, just like they're still doing now! They didn't realise that the Germans had retreated.

We went to pick some men up and one turned out to be my brother – his arm was shot away and his backside was shot away. No one was able to do anything for him at the advanced dressing station or the main dressing station so we had to go right back to the general hospital.

Part of Harry Bell's Bravery Award

"Back at the front the next day I picked up his two mates from the Enniskillen Fusiliers, At this point we had help from the American Field services as we couldn't get the ambulances to the front any more. Often they were professors and doctors doing their 6 month national service and going back to America. On one occasion one professor was very nervous and wanted to stop the ambulances and get out if there was shelling. We had to make him stay and get the patients back.

"The American ambulances were very narrow with two stretchers on the top and a bracket each side for one of the stretcher arms and a strap to hold the other. There was only a small space between them. The other two stretchers were on the floor of the ambulance. Even if the men were badly wounded and bleeding, you couldn't get in to dress them or anything, not until you got to the advanced dressing station and if they had no room there you'd have to take them all the way to the general hospital. On one occasion by the time we got there, the doctors knew that there was only one who would live out of the four. In our ambulances there was a seat at the back so that you could attend to their wounds.

"On another occasion we went over to check on an ambulance that had been tipped over and in the 10 minutes we were away, a shell came over and there was a big hole where we had been.

"So it was, we landed up in Austria to be demobbed. A colonel found out that my last leave had been June 1942"

*Jim was in the same unit as **Jim Smillie** whose marriage to a Rudry girl was described in Chapter 1. Having fought his way up through Italy and taken part in the battle of Monte Casino, perhaps it is not surprising that he was never able to talk about his war experiences.*

CHAPTER EIGHT : THE INDIAN ARMY SOLDIERS

None of the Indian Army soldiers remained in the area after the War and nobody seems to have kept in touch with them for any length of time. There are just one or two photographs.

Tom Grocutt

However, the Indian soldiers caused a great sensation in the area. **Tom Grocutt**, *then aged four, remembered seeing them arrive at Machen station.*

"There was a flurry of activity and our normal ordinary village routine was disturbed with children running about saying 'There's a troop train in the station!' I followed my elder sister down Station Hill. There was a crowd of children and adults all along the picket fence, so I found myself a little space to look through the slats and saw ramps coming down from railway trucks in the siding where the coal trucks usually unloaded, and horses slipping and sliding down the ramps into the yard. It was a very busy scene. There were lots of khaki turbans and a big bearded man on a horse who rode past very near to me. I'm almost sure he had a lance in his hand, with perhaps a little coloured pennant on top. It was all chaos and I don't know how magnified my impressions were, but the hooves of the horses seemed to be making great thuds as they went down the slope towards the main road.

"The excitement was over in about half an hour but it kept us talking for weeks! We didn't know it was anything to do with war. We were too young to worry about things like that, but later on we learnt that it was just after Dunkirk and soldiers were being sent to Ruperra from all over the place"

John Rowlands, then a schoolboy, remembered the Indian soldiers bringing three or four strings of horses through Machen, up the Dranllwyn and over the mountain for training. "One afternoon as I arrived back for afternoon school, a mule came galloping down the Dranllwyn. He'd broken loose and everybody was running out of his way. I got hold of the rope that was loose but he took me down to Ted Harris's shop before I could stop him! Then the soldier that had lost him came back with a horse to look for him and I handed him over.

"When I got back down to school I was a quarter of an hour late and I had the cane for it. That's how I remember it so well. They half believed me, but not entirely, and although someone said they'd heard that I'd stopped the runaway horse, I never had an apology and I had a good two across the hands for it.

*In No 3 The Row in Draethen, **Doris Oram** would see*

"a whole troop of Indian soldiers riding down the road exercising their lovely black horses. The road would be full of them."

Part of the Row Draethen

***Winifred Knibbs**, who lived along the Ruperra Drive in Park Wall Cottage, said*

"all of us neighbours used to visit each other. As children we'd do the rounds and go down to Mrs Blackburn's in the Preserve. The Indian soldiers would be cooking out in the open air. Some nights, when we were walking home from school across the park, they would come galloping along the path like nothing I'd ever seen before, stampeding along one behind the other. We used to have to jump into the wall to get out of the

81

way. I think this was the route they took to exercise their horses because they always used to come right across the track and then down the avenue of oaks and then back round to where they were camped."

Roy Hawkins remembered the Indian Army soldiers camped with their tents and horses between the wall and the trees just below Preserve Cottage .

"There was a big white gate with steps by the side of it on the south of the path. On one occasion when I visited, six or seven of them had a glass jar, something like a demi john and three parts full of water. On the top was an egg cup shape with tobacco in it and a stem coming out, and they were passing this jar round. I didn't know what it was at the time and they wanted me and my friends to have a drag at it. But there was no way I was going to try it."

The Indians' encampment field

John Hicks from Machen remembered the Indian soldiers wearing tight boots and jodhpurs, with a dark top coat.

John Hicks in 1948

"We boys used to go down over the lovely cobbled path at the bottom of Craig Ruperra where there was a fence made out of tree trunks cut in half, which was covered with rhododendrons. There was also a steel fence of round rods and a small gate, through which you went into the orchard and then to Preserve Cottage.

"We used to watch the Indian soldiers making chapattis. There was enough room for three people to stand around what seemed like a big bake stone resting on four steel rods, with coal glowing

82

underneath. When they put it on, the mixture was like oatmeal and they'd spread it with their fingers and turn the chapattis by throwing them up in the air. Then, when each one was cooked, they'd stack them up on a big steel plate and take them to a big marquee where all their tables and benches were laid out.

"Their sleeping quarters were in the same sort of tent but with divisions and camp beds in there. The horses were under canvas further up the track, but they used to tie them out in the day and I think they had a feeding tent for them there as well."

Herbie Spring *used always to come home to the Draethen*
"with a handkerchief full of chapattis and sugar. It was easy for us to walk up past the Hollybush, over the top and down past the Castle to the Preserve and straight into the woods where the Indian soldiers were camped."

Bernard Spooner *said*
"The Indian soldiers at the castle used to make us children very welcome". "The first chapatti I ever tasted was down there! What we used to love was the tea they made for us using condensed milk! They'd make it in brilliantly clean stainless steel buckets, and we used to love this sweet smelling, sweet tasting tea because of course for us, sugar was rationed."

Dennis Gooding *from the Waterloo, remembers, as a fourteen year old boy, seeing*

"lots of Indian soldiers and hundreds of horses camped in the trees further up from the Preserve in the field on the west side of the castle. They were good to us boys. A lot of them spoke English and so they could converse with us. They rode the horses and used the mules to carry the packs."

*Another local boy, **Albert (Ally) Griffiths**, remembered an Indian soldier coming to his house in Waterloo.*

"My father was able to speak some Indian languages after his time in the 1914-18 War so, when the Indian soldiers came to the Castle and went to the Greenmeadow Pub on their horses for a drink, he got friendly with one of the sergeants. One Saturday night, when my mother answered a knock at the door, there was the Indian sergeant stood there with his turban on and a big black beard! She couldn't see my father because he was hiding round the side. He had invited him home for supper."

Ally Griffiths today

Eric Coleman, a Machen boy, remembered getting friendly with some of the Indian soldiers.
"They were very nice people and I was invited to a meal with them. I found that they were not used to being treated as equals. They had obviously been brought up as subservient people and as such they clicked their heels and put their hands together and bowed when they spoke to you. We used to say 'you don't have to do that to us, you know, we're all in it together.' But of course it was the tail end of the Raj."

**Eric Coleman
In 1940**

**Two Indian soldiers but probably a
horse not a mule.**

CHAPTER NINE : THE PRINCESS IRENE BRIGADE

A battalion of Dutch soldiers, the 'Princess Irene Brigade' were stationed at Ruperra Castle between the 29th August and the 10th October 1940. Here is an extract from the diary of one of the Dutch soldiers, written originally in Dutch and translated into English by one of his daughters, Doctor Marietta Elliott, who lives in Australia. Another daughter, Elisabeth Anholt was on holiday in this country from Israel and emailed me after calling at Caerphilly Tourist Information Centre to enquire about the castle where her father was stationed during the war.

*Sergeant **Siegmund Emanuel Kleerkoper** had been trapped in England by the outbreak of war and, unable to return to the continent, had joined up with a contingent of Dutch nationals. After training in Congleton, in the North of England, he was sent to Ruperra. Subsequently stationed in Ceylon and India he spent the remainder of the war from September 1942, in Australia, and was attached to the Dutch Command in the Dutch East Indies after the war. His diary was addressed to his wife Hanna. His reaction to receiving the postcard from her highlights the tremendous anxieties about their families that soldiers from occupied countries felt, anxieties from which we in Britain, for the most part, were spared.*

"On the 30th of August we, the new recruits (there were about 500) moved to a large castle in Lower Machen, South Wales, named Ruperra Castle, situated a few miles from the Bristol Channel. Our Company was housed in a small building that had been a coach house. We were in the coach house itself, others in the stables, which were equipped for military accommodation. We had bunks of 4 men, two next to each other and two above. It was very agreeable there, a large dormitory, with 40 boys, we laughed a lot at the stories they told about their adventures. At night there was activity in the air over Cardiff, Newport and the convoys in the Bristol Channel, but no-one paid much attention. Tuesday was training exercises, weapons training, field exercises and, above all, marching. There, in the mountains of South Wales, I learnt to march. I could not keep up; I had large blisters under my feet and the sweat poured off my face and body. But I never gave up and I finished every march.

"At night there were bus services to take us to Cardiff and we went to the cinema or to a good restaurant. At that time the food in the camp was such that everyone had diarrhoea at night and if you were lying in bed and listened sympathetically to the shuffling through the courtyard and the room, and you were glad that you had escaped, you had to leap out of bed suddenly yourself, and run to the latrines, glad that you had made it. Most people didn't get that far, and just as you were lying in bed, relieved, you had to get up again, and so it continued. In the beginning we ate as little hot camp food as possible and ate in the city when we could. Consequently, in the camp, huge quantities were thrown away, and that earned us a lecture from the major, that we had to consider how the people in Holland had to live, and how we were sitting by the fleshpots of Egypt. This became a byword in the camp when the food was intolerable. Gradually the food improved. It did provide material for whingeing, (and if a Dutch soldier is not whingeing he is ill), but it was not taken so seriously. The surroundings were splendid, Cardiff was a pleasant city and Newport was also a nice little town, quite close, so we could manage.

"We remained there, in Ruperra Castle, for two months. We didn't have much criticism about our training, we understood that there was a shortage of weapons, and although we were very keen to learn to shoot, we were forced to practice with guns from a fairground. Most of the instructors were from the military police. Discipline was not so strict, but we had the feeling that we were learning something and doing something. We were a bit impatient at times, and annoyed with those boys who were always complaining, who lost their temper and dragged up hidden ailments or their pacifism, so that they did not acquire military knowledge, but we were not dissatisfied.

"My best memories of Ruperra Castle are, of course, first of all, the postcard I received from you. I will never forget that moment, so ordinary, as if nothing had happened, a postcard with the message that everything was fine. I had to tell and show everyone, it was a real celebration.

"In Ruperra Castle there were good opportunities to play, there was a hall with a piano, and musicians in the regiment met up there. It was there that we gave our first performance, with resounding success, for the soldiers.

"We remained in Ruperra till two days before Yom Kippur, 1940. From there we departed for Conwy in North Wales, near some famous beach resorts such as Rhyl, Colwyn Bay and Llandudno, in splendid surroundings, mountainous and on the coast."

*Some of the Dutch soldiers described in the account above had escaped from Holland before the Germans invaded and had landed at Milford Haven. Six or seven weeks later, they came to Ruperra. It was the first time that **Bernard Spooner** had heard a foreign language in Draethen*

"The first time they came down through the woods from Ruperra to Draethen, they were thrilled to find, in the garden of Mrs Lloyd's teashop in the Row, orange marigolds which they thought had been planted specially for them. We children were told that the colour orange had been banned in Holland by the Germans because the Dutch Royal Family were the House of Orange. So they each took one and put it in their Glengarry caps, and in one night that bed of marigolds had disappeared."

The Row today

CHAPTER 10 : FIRE AND DESTRUCTION DECEMBER 6TH 1941

So many people can remember exactly where they were and what they were doing when they heard the news that Ruperra Castle was on fire. The following morning came the news of the Japanese attack on Pearl Harbour.

Ethel Ackland, *noticed that there was no water coming out of the tap outside her house. Then she saw how pink the sky was.* "I could see the flames coming out in a square from the castle. You can imagine with the height of it, the flames coming out like a square fire place and out through the windows.

Ethel and Bill Ackland

"I went up the drive to look. Bill was getting over pneumonia and didn't like it much that he had to stay with the children. There were a lot of people there before me. It was well on the way then. It was a windy wet night and that I think saved us from bombing otherwise with the Castle all lit up like that we'd have had bombs as well. It was terrible. The flames were coming out through the windows. I could hear the crackling of all the varnish and polish in the wood I suppose. I never want to see that again. I was never frightened of fire before that. I would be now.

"Of course there was a black out as well. There were fire engines stuck all over the place. One was in Coed y Gwineu. Some of them didn't get to the castle at all. If they'd had a raid in Cardiff that night they'd have been in trouble. Some engines must have got there because we didn't have any water in our house. They drained all the water in the pond as well. They were playing the hoses on the houses and the outbuildings because they couldn't do anything for the Castle."

Bernard Spooner, who lived further away in Machen, can remember seeing the glow in the sky and the sparks flying up into the air.

"Everybody thought the Castle had been hit by German bombers, mistaking the larchwoods around Ruperra for the camouflage of Rogerstone Aluminium Works. Of course, as we know, there were clouds that night, and therefore no bombing raids, because if the German bombers had been up to Birmingham or Coventry and were coming back down this way, they used to dump their bombs anywhere.

Bernard Spooner

"There was a story of there being a huge fire extinguishing system in the castle, a huge water tank in the roof with chains hanging down the walls. People said that if these chains had been pulled they would have released the water but nobody knew about it, although a lot of people wondered what the chains were for. In any case no doubt they'd all rusted up, and never been checked or tested. They didn't save the Castle anyway."

Roy Hawkins described the Castle as being "like a huge blowlamp. My Uncle Stradling, who was up at the Griffin having a pint, said that you could read an Echo even up there by the light of the Castle burning, it was so bright.

Doris Oram *and her husband, working nights at the 'Rodgy' works, the Rodgerston Aluminium factory, were in bed in No. 3 The Row in Draethen.* "It was nearly time for us to get up to go to work and we heard the fire engines rushing up the road to the Michaelstone entrance to the Castle. We were sure the Germans had invaded because of the row the fire engines were making. We can laugh about it now but at the time it was very frightening."

*The first that **Colin Anstey**, up at Rhyd y Gwern Farm, knew of the fire was that,*
"somebody phoned about it. We had just had the telephone in the house then. I remember the light in the sky; it was just like day down there. We never went down possibly because it was such a terrible night, pouring with rain. There was more rain came down on that castle than what the firemen put on it. But we only had to go outside the front door and you could see every bit of it.

"I was told that Mr Blackburn, the old keeper from Preserve Cottage, had gone up to the castle and told the driver of the first engine to follow him to the pond down the hard road on the Cardiff drive, but they couldn't wait for him. They could see the water in the reflection of the fire and they cut off across the grass. They only went 20 yards before they stuck in the soft earth and couldn't go any further."

Herbie Spring *had been to Newport.*
"The last bus out of town in those days used to be about a quarter to ten. You could see the reflection of the flames in the clock face up on the top on the old station approach alongside the old general post office. I know there is a big hill between Newport and Ruperra, but the clock was high enough to reflect the fire. We didn't know what it was but as we came nearer we could see that there was a big fire. We went up there the following day but of course there were soldiers stopping you going further than the driveway."

David Jones, *of Glan-y-Nant Farm, thought that all the buildings would have gone if it had been a dry windy night.* "But it was a damp miserable old night. We all went up the drive to see it. There were loads of people up there. You could see it from miles around. But then they had no water, only the duck pond, or something. They had several Brigades up there but I don't think they could do a lot of good to it because they were short of water. It was late evening and it was going well when we went up there. There was a soldier, courting a girl from Cardiff who used to leave his motor bike here who said that the wiring was very poor, and that it was not a bit of wonder that it went on fire."

Dennis Gooding was fourteen then and remembered, "somebody coming and saying 'The castle's on fire!' and we ran, two or three of us from Machen, up through the woods behind the Hollybush and stood on the bank watching it and it was all in flames."

Eight year old Dennis Penny did the same from Ruperra Park Lodge. "I can remember the fire engines going past our house one after another and I could see the flames. We went up the footpath in the woods behind the Castle to look at it from there."

Terry Everson from Machen had been to the pictures in Bedwas Hall with her eldest sister. They had gone to the second house. She said "coming out then at a quarter past 10, there being no bus at that time, we were walking home. Coming down the hill towards Trethomas, we could see this orange and gold glare in the sky, massive. It would flare up bright and then it would dull a bit, but go on and on. There'd be this awful build up and blow out and all these sparks, just as if something was exploding and spewing out into this orange glow. It was like that all the way home to Wesley Hill in Machen, which was a good two and a half miles.

Terry Everson 1940s

"We didn't know until the Sunday morning on the 7th December 1941 that Ruperra Castle had been burnt down again. That was the second time for it to burn down because although of course nobody remembered the fire of 1793 everybody knew about it."

91

People know that soldiers were at the castle when it burnt down but over the years all sorts of myths have grown up. It is often said with great confidence that the Americans were responsible. However the fire was raging on the night of 6th December when Japanese planes started their journey towards Pearl Harbour. It was only then that America entered the war. Italian prisoners of war have also been blamed but it is doubtful if there were ever any Italian prisoners of war at Ruperra. They were at Castleton later. The Dutch were also blamed, but as we have seen they left the Castle in October 1940.

When Tony Friend wrote his book, 'Lord Tredegar's Ruperra Castle' in 1985 he received a letter from **Lance Robinson**, one of the 307 Searchlight Regiment. It is printed here and explains everything.

> Lance Robinson
> 22 Yeoman Street
> North Shields
> North Tyneside
> NE29 6NL.
>
> Ruperra Castle.
>
> Dear Sir,
>
> A Welsh friend of mine who lives now, in my home town, has shown me a photo of your model of "RUPERRA CASTLE".
>
> I know that we "Geordies" speak a special kind of language but to be taken for "Dutchmen" comes as a bit of a surprise. What I mean is that we were British Soldiers that were there, the night the Castle took fire not the poor "dutch" who seem to be blamed for it.
>
> The fire brigades came from all over South Wales, even from

England, I remember, I sent a cutting from the Newspaper to my Dad, of the facts of the episode. The officer who was injured was one of local Rugby Union players, from Tyneside.

After the fire we had to live in the stables.

The castle was beautiful - the grand room upstairs had a spring floor for dancing I presume (although I can not remember a dance). The men who had been billeted in the castle were very upset, the day after the fire, to see the place gutted.

As far as we knew the fire started in the attics, and some of the lads who could not get out by the staircase owing to the rafters falling on to the stairs, had to lower themselves out of the upstairs windows. My brother and

I came out that way, also our pet dog "Taffy" who behaved wonderfully well.

The Officer who visited us, after the fire, I was told was Lord Tredegar. He seemed very concerned regarding the comfort of the soldiers.

I am very sorry to see that the Castle has been left to neglect, as I used to love to look around it, and the surrounding area. The locals were very nice people and I liked the club.

I hope this letters puts the facts right

Yours Truly

Lance Robinson
Ex Sgt R.Es

P.S. Is there not a report in the South Wales Argus regarding the fire.

RUPERRA CASTLE GUTTED

—:❋:—

RUPERRA Castle, stately Seventeenth Century home for generations of successive Lords Tredegar, was gutted by fire during the night of Saturday-Sunday.

Newport Fire Brigade, assisted by neighbouring brigades, fought the flames throughout the night, but were unable to save the castle.

There is an old prophecy, of which those most closely associated with the Tredegar Estate have heard which says that Ruperra would be burned down three times.

This is the second time in its long, colourful history that Ruperra Castle has been destroyed by fire. It was burned down in 1783, when very little but the outer walls was left standing. That fact was recorded on a stone which was placed in the dining-room when the Castle was restored in 1789.

Recently, Ruperra Castle was occupied by the military. Troops were there when the fire started. Some, trapped in the upper parts of the Castle, made dramatic escapes. One soldier, cut off by the flames, jumped from the third storey to the quadrangle, fifty feet below, and was severely injured. Four firemen were also hurt, none seriously, though one fireman, who lowered himself by means of a rope, fell and fractured a leg.

STARTED IN ROOF

How Saturday's fire started is unknown. It was first discovered in the roof, and spread very quickly. For a time, gallant efforts were made to control the flames with stirrup-pumps, but these were unavailing.

When the Fire Brigades reached the scene, the castle was a mass of flames. The blaze was fought throughout the night by more than a hundred firemen. Soon, the roof crashed.

The famous banqueting hall was completely wrecked; its massive oak beams hung weirdly out of a mountain of debris.

MAJESTIC STRUCTURE

Nearly four hundred feet above sea level, Ruperra was a majestic, three-storey structure, with battlemented towers and parapet rising to a great height. It was in this beautiful mansion, on the borders of Monmouthshire and Glamorgan, that the late Lord Tredegar entertained many guests, but apart from occasional visits by guests, the castle was subsequently unoccupied for some time.

Its story is full of romance. The porch bore the date 1622, and history records that it was built by "one Sir Thomas Morgan," a cousin of the then head of the family, Sir William Morgan, who lived at Tredegar House.

Sir Thomas, a strong Royalist, once had the honour of entertaining the hard-pressed King Charles I. after the defeat at Naseby.

An element of mystery surrounded the identity of the designer of the Castle, but records claim it as one of the works of Inigo Jones. One of the features of it (up to the time of the War, the Castle's lofty rooms contained many treasures of art, which then were removed), was a great staircase, a fine example of Georgian architecture. This is now a blackened ruin.

One of its treasures was a large collection of pikes, which belonged to the old West Monmouthshire local Militia, which had a company of pikemen in 1800.

The late Lord Tredegar loved the old building. He spent his boyhood there and later, recalling incidents of that time, related how he was out with his terrier when the post boy, who had been sent into Newport to get letters, rode back pale and quivering, flung himself from his pony, and said the Chartists were in Newport. The future Lord Tredegar is stated to have retorted: "Bother your Chartists; come and help me catch this rabbit."

In one corner of the ground floor was the favourite sitting-room of the late Colonel F. C. Morgan, M.P., a fine old sportsman.

Those who were privileged to visit the Castle in the days of its glory were greatly impressed by the beauty of a Minstrels' Gallery, a unique work.

The oak panelling, outstanding of its kind, was valued at a very high figure. All that is now destroyed.

Ruperra was the birthplace of Godfrey Charles Morgan, the first Viscount Tredegar, of Balaclava fame. The present Viscount Tredegar's father was also born there.

South Wales Argus December 9th 1941

Lance was sure that

"Only our Regiment of about 50 men was in Ruperra when it burnt down. The rest had gone out on to the searchlight sites. They reckoned there was an electrical fault. The Castle hadn't been used, you see, and so when all the lights went on, the electric wires in the ceilings and the walls were overloaded. I mean, if you'd smoked a cigarette in the Castle you couldn't have set fire to it because there was no furniture or anything to catch. It wasn't our neglect. You're not going to burn your own home down are you? We'd been in some big places before and they'd been all right.

"The fire started in the ceilings. They were falling in and everybody was trying to get down the stairs. That's why we jumped out through the windows. There was a scatter, just a big scatter. A fellow came in to where the men were sleeping or playing cards and said in Geordie 'Away - the hiss took a hardin' which means 'Get out, the house is on fire'. There was a cockney lad who used to do all the cleaning, who went round outside throwing pieces of coal in through the windows of the separate rooms with officers and sergeants in. The rest of us had been together in the large rooms.

"The whole aim was to get everybody outside and then see what you could do. You couldn't do anything inside. There was a roll call to check that everyone was out. It was probably about 9 or 10 o'clock when the fire started and by 1 or 2 o'clock in the morning it was well away, burning itself out. It was dark you know and people could see the flames all around the area. There were some hoses got out of the outhouses and we were told to hold on to them tight because they kick. But there was no water coming out of them.

"The fire brigades came from Cardiff, Newport, all over the place, but they couldn't all get through. And when they did, it was too late. The following day Lord Tredegar came in his brass hat - he wasn't in a proper army dress, it was an honorary one. He said he was very glad that we'd all got out.

96

"Lieutenant Barker, a very nice fellow, went in to rescue the mascot dog, a bulldog, called Tyne. It was frightened by the fire and went back into the Castle. There were friction hoists above the windows which he used to lower the dog so he couldn't use it for himself and had to jump from the second floor. He broke both his legs and of course that finished him in the Army. He was a Rugby player too."

They all slept in a big room above the stables after that. Lance remembers that Pat Kirkwood was supposed to come to do an Ensa show in the Banqueting Hall but with it being burnt down she gave it in the stables. Eventually Lance went inside the Castle. He remembers seeing all the inside flattened. When he looked up he could see the sky

"Ruperra had been really something for someone like me to see. The rooms there were fancy and there was a sprung floor in the hall on the first floor. We'd seen castles before, we've got a lot of castles up here on Tyneside you know, but this was really beautiful. And I've never forgotten the chandelier. When it was all over I was really upset. The surroundings were so nice, the gardens and the trees. I enjoyed it there and I'm sorry for those who never had the chance to see it as it was."

Ray Neville, from the same regiment, said he was on the site at Bulmore when he heard that the Castle had burnt down.

"I was very saddened. It was unbelievable really. Apparently it was an electrical fault which caused it all. I think they might have had power on the bottom floors and wanted to get power on other floors. Probably when they switched the power on to these floors there was an electrical short circuit which started the fire in the ceilings and under the floorboards and with it being dry, it just got away and went up very quickly."

Andy Newton remarked that "there were probably only about 60 of us there at the time, so I can't see how the wiring got overloaded to start the fire. We always went into the Castle by the West entrance, then up the stairs to the top of the building. The main thing you noticed when you went up the stairs to the part where we were billeted, was all the fire hoses and even fire axes. Looking back this was what amazed me, that every floor had all these fire extinguishers and hoses, with rising butts bolted down, and at every window there was one of these arms that swung out in case of fire. Of course, we used to query this with the locals, and they said that the castle had been burned down before. It was after this that all these fire escapes had been put in. I never remember having a fire drill there, although of course I was only there a fortnight before the fire. I just couldn't believe how the whole place had been burnt down.

"The night of the fire, I happened to be on leave in South Shields. My uncle used to come every morning to my house and we'd go out. I'd been telling them about the marvellous billet I had, how we were living like kings there and how it was such a nice place. Anyway he came this one morning and said 'That's a lovely billet you've got there!' I said 'Yes, its fantastic!' He said 'It *was,* it's been burnt to the ground last night!' Now he was a big joker so I didn't really believe him. Then I saw it in the paper.

"When I got back off leave and saw the state of it, it was terrible to look at after seeing it in its prime. The workmanship that was in the place would be difficult to replace.

"All the boys had lost all their kit in the fire, some of them all their personal belongings. I still had all my kit because when you went on leave, you used to pack it all up and put it in the stores on one of the floors in the stable block. After the fire, of course, we were all sleeping in the Stable Block, on the top floor.

"As for the cause of the fire, a special Army body was sent to investigate and the report said that it was an electrical fault. If it had been our fault, the Unit would have had to pay towards it. We had had money deducted from our pay when we came back from France, for the damage some of the men had done in Aldershot barracks before leaving. Basically, the normal procedure when there are two sets of electrical plant is to run one plant one week while you're servicing the other. The generators were probably designed to supply just so much current for the Castle, not expecting every floor to be lit up as happened when the Army was there.

Possibly the two generators were run at the same time to double the output, thus causing the overloading.

"After Ruperra, we went to Druidstone House. One of the lodges on the St. Mellons side also caught fire only two or three weeks after we went there. Only the sergeants were billeted inside the lodge. The entertainments officer we had at that time formed a little dance band called the 'Fire Raisers!' The boys painted flames on the big drum and the stands for the music had flames painted on as well."

Henry Whitnell's father was the Fire Station Officer at Caerphilly when Ruperra Castle caught fire. Henry, aged 17, was the station messenger, with a motor bike. Since the younger firemen had gone to the War, most of those who attended the fire were much older and unfortunately are no longer alive. Sadly, Henry himself died in 2000.

Caerphilly's "new" 1938 Fire Engine, now in a museum in the Midlands.

"It was about 6 o'clock in the evening when we had the call to Ruperra Castle. We set off from the fire station in Mill Road, in this brand spanking new machine which my father had just had delivered from

Coventry. Somebody said, 'How do you get to Ruperra Castle?' The answer was, 'Don't bother, we can see it! As we were coming along Van Road you could see the flames in the sky, and as we went up past the Maenllwyd you could see the roof blazing away. It was already gone.

"I can still remember the feeling of being very inadequate when we pulled into the yard of Ruperra Castle. It happened to me many times after Ruperra, but this was the first. There was the new engine, which now looked awfully small by the side of this huge blazing building, five firemen, me on a motorcycle and no water. There were some soldiers there in the yard manning a hose on a standpipe. The water was just trickling out of the pipe. The place seemed enormous. The fire was going right up through the roof. The castle was already doomed. What the hell were we going to do with this?

"People often wonder why the fire was so advanced when the call was first put out. I think the soldiers probably tried to put it out themselves instead of calling the fire brigade.

"There were no radios on fire engines in those days so my job was to take a message back to the station on my motor cycle. On this occasion, however, they had put a ladder up against the side of the building, where there was a telephone right by the window. My father smashed one of the little panes (the fire was already at the other side of the room) and actually put out the call for assistance from the place that was on fire. So appliances were arriving at the station wanting instructions when I got back and I guided the first convoy to the fire.

"The firemen were told that the nearest water supply was a lake down in a field below the Castle so they took the engine down there dumping hose off all the way but the ground was so boggy that she sank in the mud before she got to the water. So they continued running the hose out by hand. By the time they'd got the hose completely run out, the trailer pumps were already arriving with the Newport and Cardiff City engines.

"The trailer pumps weighed about a ton and were normally pulled behind a towing vehicle, but because the ground was so soft, the firemen were having to unhitch them and manhandle them down to the water. The

100

engine of the bogged down Caerphilly machine was kept running and used as part of the relay of pumps pumping water all the way up the field from pump to pump in order to keep the pressure up. There were 3 lines of pumps eventually, running from the pond across the field to the Castle.

"Fire Brigades from Bargoed and Aberbargoed all got to the yard. They came with trailer pumps but they couldn't use the hose pipes in the Castle yard because there was no water pressure. They put a lightweight pump on the standpipe there to try and boost the pressure, but the water kept stopping all the time. The wells under the Castle were too deep. Theoretically, a pump can pump water at 34 feet down but in fact 27 feet is the furthest it can pick it up. If you drop a suction pump down into a well, the moment it gets below 27 feet you can't pick water up any more. So wells are not a lot of good really. It was down the field or nothing. We pumped the pond practically dry. The fire was just about dying when the pumps down there started to take in air.

"The fact that the Castle was so heavily timbered hadn't helped. The firemen broke through into the Banqueting Hall just as its roof collapsed.

The Banqueting Hall after the fire.

Father's uniform was like a colander when he got home, all holes. The firemen confined the fire to the main building with the water that they managed to get, and formed a barrier with the turntable ladders between the Castle and the other buildings.

"After the fire it took an awful lot of trouble to get all the equipment from there. There were 3 tractors and 150 men pulling the Caerphilly machine out of the mud. She'd actually sunk in such a way that her back end was at an angle and the mud was up to the rear doors. It took three days to get the 14 ton turntable ladders away from there, because by now the lanes had collapsed under the weight of the vehicles.

"Although we had realised when we got there that we couldn't save the Castle, the fire had to be put out quickly because it was wartime and it would have been a beacon for enemy aircraft. We were there all night long and half the following day. The fire subsided in the early hours of the morning. It had burnt itself out by then. All the insides had collapsed in a big heap. It smouldered for days."

The fire engine was brought from its museum to Henry Whitnell's house in Caerphilly in 1989, when his father, aged 93 was visiting him.

CHAPTER 11 : RUPERRA SOLDIERS AFTER THE FIRE

*When **Roy Chapman** came to Ruperra, the castle was already burnt down. He said it was rumoured that it was the NAAFI chappie that had got in trouble with his accounts! While Roy was there, his wife and little daughter came to stay in Draethen with Fred and Doris Oram.*

Roy Chapman in his cook's uniform

"I had gone down to Southampton and they picked fifty of us out, trained us to be cooks and distributed us to different places. We'd had all our inoculations and everything for going abroad but I was sent to Ruperra! Then, after we'd trained the various units at Ruperra, they'd be sent off to other places.

"At Ruperra, in the cookhouse, we had six ovens standing back-to-back, coal fired. Sometimes when we were training at Ruperra there'd be four or five hundred men to feed each day. The number of men I had working under me varied. I had six regular trainers, but sometimes when another unit came in they'd bring two or three cooks with them, ready trained. The people who worked there, slept upstairs in the Stable Block but those people who came in, in different units, to be trained, had tents and huts.

"All nationalities came but the Irish were the best workers of the lot! There were Canadians and Americans there when I was there. We had one chappie that I got friendly with who had been in the German Army. Over here he went by the name of Burton. He told me that he'd got a wife and daughter over in Germany but that he daren't try and get in touch with them. He'd spent four days in a cornfield when he deserted from the German Army. He was a very genuine fellow. He had had to go through lots of tests. He told me that he hadn't known what name to take and he'd looked out of the window of the bus and seen the name of Burton's Tailors and thought he'd have that one.

"Once, we had a shortage of fuel for the ovens at Ruperra. But there was about 10 ton of coal dust there. So I got a bag of cement from the stores and I got the chaps making blocks, and laid them out alongside the wall to dry

"The cookhouse was in the Stable Block. There was a stone staircase to go up to the sleeping quarters. Four of us slept in one of the smaller rooms on proper double decker bunk beds which were really comfortable. There was a big old tortoiseshell stove in it - the sort you bank up with coke and they go for ages. One afternoon, when it had begun to get a bit cold, I cleaned it out and lit it. When the chaps came in one of them said 'Who lit that fire? I've got a bar of chocolate in my kit bag. I think it's melted it!' - and it had!

"The officers had a mess in the room on the left of the stable block as you go in. They had separate sleeping quarters in some portable buildings just over in the park, the other side of the wall (where the orchard used to be). I cooked for Captain Brown, and his batman Corporal Towel used to come and get it. The other officers had their own cookhouse.

"The food we provided was excellent. Captain Brown and Mr Ford the farmer were friendly, so we weren't short of anything! The Home Guard from Cardiff used to come and pitch their tents in the field in the park and they used to bring most of their food into the cookhouse for me to cook for them. I think I ran the cookhouse well. Phillip Rye the actor, who was Captain of the Catering Corps told me one day that he thought I had the best cookhouse in the British Army.

"For breakfast, the men had bacon and egg, and there was always plenty of bread because we were next door to the Bakery, and there was always jam. We managed to vary the food. You'd never have the same thing

104

twice in a week Supplies were collected from the Catering Supplies Depot in Newport and kept in a big store up in one corner of the Square, on the ground floor of the Stable Block, opposite the stables. There were no horses there. The storeroom was kept locked up and there was no problem with rats. They were kept down by Captain Brown's cat - it was as big as a dog - a monster.

"There was one old chappie, he'd been in the Army for years - I was surprised he was still in the forces he was so old, but he was an experienced man. He used to stand by the door in the morning when the chaps came in for their breakfast and pick them out. 'Go and get a wash!' 'I'll miss my breakfast, Sir!' 'Too bad! Go and get a wash. You should have got up sooner and had one before you came.' He knew he had to be like that. They'd have got the upper hand of him otherwise.

"I remember Tom Pembridge, the caretaker, very well. He used to be about early in the mornings. He used to drop in the cookhouse for a cup of tea. I remember one day I picked his mint that he'd been trying to grow for ages. I wanted some to go with the lamb we had. I didn't know how precious it was to him! He had been in charge of the boiler, feeding it all the time to keep the water hot, but it got too much for him, he couldn't keep up with it so the soldiers started to do it.

Roy Chapman in 2000

"It was really interesting being at Ruperra and what I liked about it was when I had my time off in the day time I could walk all round everywhere. I used to walk to Cefn Mably. I knew my way around very well. What amazed me, having lived in the country myself, was how so many fellows were afraid to come up through the woods on their own. They'd wait down there in Draethen for over half an hour for somebody else to come. I was going up there one night and heard something rustling about in the leaves and thought

'What the devil's that?' So I stood still right up against a tree and a badger came up to within touching distance before it smelt me. Then of course it shot off.

"I was married before the War. Our daughter Valerie was two when the war broke out and she went to school in Machen, when she and her mother were staying with the Orams." *Valerie said that it was so silly that the only thing she could remember was going across the field, over a stile and through the wood to the Castle. But her impression of those days was that* 'everybody used to help one another. Nowadays you don't really know your neighbours.' *Doris Oram remembered coming home from work and finding that Valerie's mother had done all her cleaning for her and cooked the meal.*

Roy said

"I enjoyed being at Ruperra. It was 'country'. I know that when some of us were asked to go and Captain Brown asked me if I wanted to go or stay. I said 'I'll stay if I've got the choice!' He said 'What, in a place like this?' I said 'It's a lovely place. I'm country, bred and born, I'd hate to go in the town.' 'Oh well,' he said, 'if that's how you feel about it, you can certainly stay.' So that's how I stayed there so long. It was very pleasant there, a marvellous place to be."

In 1945, by the time **Norman Baxter** *went back to Ruperra, he'd been to Egypt, Cyprus, Ceylon and India.* "On V E day I was in Bury St.Edmunds baking bread for the American forces, but as I didn't want to be an instructor, they sent me to Ruperra again.

"By this time I was a sergeant and was sent to take charge of the Bakery, manned by German prisoners of war. There were about 30 prisoners, about half a dozen guards, 2 sentries and myself. I was there to do the accounts and was in charge of the Bakery, but not of the German workers. They were supervised by their camp leader, the Lager Fuhrer. He could speak English, which was just as well since I couldn't speak German. They were good workers, the Germans. Mostly ex-Navy, I think, I don't how they'd got there, but I never had anything to do with them unless I wanted them to do something. If they had a problem, the Lager Fuhrer would come to me and we'd sort it out. I wasn't there very long. I used to go round the Bakery from time to time just to see that everything was being done properly. I used to be in charge of ordering the materials. I'd have to go down to Newport every day to get the rations, in an army truck with a driver.

"This time I slept in the Stable Block, in the block of four or five rooms along the corridor at the top. There was plenty of room there because there were only a few of us. I had a proper single bed. It was comfortable - I was the governor then of course! I remember I was in the big room at the end of the corridor, with a big coal fire in a grate. It was winter time and quite a cold one, the back end of 45/46. I used to eat on my own as well, but not in the Stable Block. Someone used to cook the food for me. My office was in one of these buildings as well. There was a lady living in the rooms on the right hand side of the stables and I used to talk to her sometimes.

"Then because the unit at Hereford was being disbanded, I had to go back to Hereford to dispose of the stores and equipment there. When I left, the Germans were still there. I used to have a wooden tray that they made for me out of some panelling from the Castle, but it's gone now.

"There was barbed wire all round the camp, but there was nothing to stop the prisoners going out. The sentries used to stand guard at the main entrance, but wouldn't see them going out over the very low wall at the back of the Castle. That's the way I went when I used to walk around the outside of the wall on Sunday afternoons. It's a long walk round the Estate. One night I took a wrong turning. That was an even longer walk! We used to walk through the woods to go to the local pubs. I enjoy walking, I always have done. I enjoy the country. I liked it at Ruperra."

Ernest Harvey returned from the Burma Campaign at the end of the war and was sent to Ruperra castle where they were short of men to look after the German prisoners of war. They stayed at Ruperra until it closed down.

"There were grapes growing against the wall of the stable block, and the caretaker was living there, a tall man. There seemed to be lots of greyhounds there.

"There were Land Army girls stationed in Nissen huts about four or five miles along the road to Michaelstone. There were two or three of our blokes courting the land army girls. At the bottom of the stairs where we had our quarters, there were big boilers where we used to do our washing and the Land Army girls laughed their heads off one day because I dunked my army vests in the boiler and when I got them out they were tiny. I'd boiled them.

Ernest Harvey in 1999

"There were about twenty or thirty prisoners in the Nissen huts in the grounds. There weren't many soldiers guarding them, and those that were, were being demobbed all the time. They made lovely white bread which we couldn't get at the time, so I used to take some home to the wife in Tintern. I also used to take sweets from the WVS van that used to pull up outside the main gates. And when the Germans made little sandals out of rope, I used to take them home as well. I used to give them fags. They weren't allowed to go outside the gates on their own, so we used to take them on route marches. But there was no worry about them really. They knew they were going home. They were demobbed from Newport Docks. They were nice people. In the room on the ground floor on the right of the stable entrance, they painted a picture of 'the Pimple' as we called it - the mountain with all the woods on it and a picnic place with a couple of benches there."

When **Roy Hawkins** returned home in March 1946, the German prisoners were still at Ruperra. "They seemed to be free to go wherever they wanted. One day, I thought I'd widen the narrow footpath down to our

108

house and started digging it out with a spade. I had got about a third of the way, when some German prisoners came along and saw me. They couldn't speak very good English but they made me understand that if I got them a shovel they'd help me. They dug the rest of it out but wouldn't take money for it, all they wanted was coffee and biscuits from my mother. But they still wanted to do something to help. There was an old rough part of the garden and my father asked them to dig that. We made them take money for that."

POST SCRIPT

Ruperra Castle in 1949 with one Nissen hut still standing

Looking back on the changes after the War, **Dorothy Jones,** *who lives in Machen, said*

'Everything was different after the War. I mean, when we were children you had to go to church on a Sunday. It was part of our lives and we used to go for walks after church in the summer, cutting across the fields and up over the Iron Bridge to the summerhouse, and sometimes we'd go straight up to the Castle and come down through the woods. That was our walk, every week. And even when I met my husband, who was from Rudry, we'd walk there from Rudry. It was part of our lives then, to go for walks.

"For as long as I can remember, we used to go and pick wild daffodils going up to the summerhouse. On the Castle side there were massive rhododendrons. On the Draethen side, in the field behind the Hollybush and both sides of the stream behind the Trout Farm, there were loads of snowdrops. It used to be white all the way up there.

"After the war, I don't think many went up to the Castle or the summerhouse any more. People got cars and of course, you weren't allowed to drive up the track at the back of the castle."

And so, as in most other places, after the war, when the soldiers, returned home, things were never the same again. People had learnt to drive in the army. They didn't go for walks in their own countryside so much. They could drive to other places now, although the pilgrimage on foot to the top of Craig Ruperra to see the tragic ruins of Ruperra Castle still continued for a while. Then in 1956 Coed Ruperra was sold as a commercial woodland.

Those men and women who hadn't had a trade before the War, had now been trained and expected to be employed. The once all-protecting, all-providing Ruperra Estate was even less able to provide employment for those returning than it had been in 1918. The castle was in ruins and the gardens, woodlands and parklands, already neglected, would never be cared for again in the same way. The planted conifers were already suffocating ancient Coed Ruperra, and it became less attractive to go there. The wooden summerhouse gradually fell to pieces, and the laurel spread without restraint and covered the mound. The grassy rides were no longer kept clear.

There was some talk in the late 1940s of the ruined castle being bought by the National Trust and made into a memorial for Welsh soldiers killed in the war. Nothing came of this, however. Evan Morgan having died in 1949, his cousin John sold the 300 acre Ruperra Estate, in 1956, to Eagle Star Insurance Company. With this, the Ruperra Estate built up over at least eight hundred years, and once such a permanent part of the structure of local life, came to an end.

111

Further Reading

Malcolm Airs,The Buildings of Britain, Tudor and Jacobean, Barrie and Jenkins 1982

Cadw / Icomos Register of Landscapes, Parks &Gardens of Special Historical Interest in Wales. UK 1998

Alexander Cresswell, The Silent Houses of Britain, Macdonald & Co 1991

G T Clark 'Limbus Patrum Morganiae et Glamorganiae' 1886

Penny David, A Garden Lost in Time, Weidenfield and Nicholson 1999

Tony Friend. Lord Tredegar's Ruperra Castle Community Design for Gwent. 1990

Mark Girouard, Robert Smythson and the Elizabethen Country House, Yale Univ. Press 1983

John B. Hilling, The Historic Architecture of Wales, Cardiff, 1976

Ian Vernon Hogg Dictionary of World War II Brockhampton Press 1994

David J Knowles Escape from Catastrophe. Knowles Publishing 2000

Thomas Lloyd, The Lost Houses of Wales SAVE Britain's Heritage 1986

Benjamin Malkin, The Scenery, Antiquities and Biography of South Wales. London 1804

Pat Moseley Memories of Coed Craig Ruperra. Ruperra Conservation Trust 1999

Serving Under Ruperra. Heritage Lottery Fund, Clarke Printing 2005

John Newman, The Buildings of Wales, Glamorgan, Penguin 1995

Roger Phillips, Tredegar, the Self Publishing Company 1990

RCAHM (W) Inventory of Ancient Monuments in Glamorgan, Vol IV, Part I The Greater Houses.1981, HMSO

Peter Smith, Houses of the Welsh Countryside, HMSO 1975

Time Tracks, Caerphilly County Borough Council's Heritage Trail 2001

Index

Photographs indicated by bold italics.

114

Penzance 60 64
Po River 78
Portadown 45 47
Preserve Cottage 67 81 *82* 90
Princess Irene Brigade 85-89
Queen Alexandra Nurses 75
Rae Albert (Forester) 71 76
Ramsgate 51
Red Cross Flag 78
Reeves Roy 26 *65*
Rhyl 54 87
Robinson Lance 50 92 -94
Rogers John (wife Betty Cage) 37 38
Rogerstone 66 67 89
Row the, Draethen *21* 71 *87*
Rowlands John 81
Royal Army Service Corps 71 76
Royal Corps of Signals 28 29 36
Royal Welsh Fusiliers 45
Rudry 10 11 110 Rudry Mill 70
Royal Army Medical Corps 47 71-75
Ruperra
        Banqueting Hall *101*
        Castle *56* 7 8 10 11 12 *14* 24 27 31 33 34 36 45 48 51 57 61 71 75
        76 85 87 88 89 91 92-4 *95* 99 *110*
        Coed Craig (Woods) 8 11 17 67 82 108 111
        Drive 81
        Estate 5 6 107 111
        Fire 7 88 – 102 Fire engine *99*
        Gardens 6 107 – 8
        Generator Block *24*
        Home Farm 19–20 68
        Park Lodge 22 33 91
        'Pimple' 105
        Stable Block *9 24* 30 62 98 103-4 105 107
Russians 35 48
Sangro 78
Scotland 76